helge rosvaenge
tiana lemnitz
franz völker
maria müller
max lorenz

singers of the third reich

5 separate discographies
compiled by john hunt

contents

3   acknowledgement

5   introduction

9   helge rosvaenge

71   tiana lemnitz

113   franz völker

189   maria müller

213   max lorenz

Singers of the Third Reich
Published by John Hunt.
Designed by Richard Chluparty
© 2001 John Hunt
reprinted 2009
ISBN 978-1-901395-08-2

Sole distributors:
Travis & Emery,
17 Cecil Court,
London, WC2N 4EZ,
United Kingdom.
(+44) 20 7 459 2129.
sales@travis-and-emery.com

acknowledgement

these publications have been made possible by contributions or advance subscriptions from

Stefano Angeloni
Yoshihiro Asada
Charles Brooke
George Burr
George Cobby
Dennis Davis
Richard Dennis
Hans-Peter Ebner*
Andrew Fox
Peter Fülöp
Jean-Pierre Goossens
Johann Gratz
Michael Harris
Naoya Hirabayashi
Martin Holland
Bodo Igesz
Detlef Kissmann
John Larsen
Elisabeth Legge-Schwarzkopf*
John Mallinson*
Carlo Marinelli
Bruce Morrison
Alessandro Nava
Hugh Palmer*
Laurence Pateman
Johann Christian Petersen
Yves Saillard
Robin Scott
Yoshihiko Suzuki*
Urs Weber*
G. Wright

Stathis Arfanis
E.C. Blake
Gordon Buffard
Edward Chibas*
Robert Dandois
F. De Vilder
John Derry
Henry Fogel*
Nobuo Fukumoto
Brian Godfrey
N. Goulty
A.C. Greenburgh
Tadashi Hasegawa*
Don Hodgman
Chris Hunt
Rodney Kempster
Bent Klovborg
Douglas MacIntosh
Norman MacDougall
Neil Mantle
Philip Moores
W. Moyle
Alan Newcombe
Jim Parsons*
James Pearson
Linda Perkins
Ingo Schwarz
Tom Scragg*
H.A. Van Dijk
Nigel Wood

*indicates life subscriber

Introduction
One of the more positive outcomes of the Second World War was the development of magnetic tape as a recording medium and the resulting preservation of a multitude of musical performances which would otherwise have disappeared into the ether after their initial broadcast. The surviving radio tape recordings of musicians in Hitler's Germany confirm and amplify what was already evident from the commercial gramophone recordings which they were making before, during and after this same period: that here was a remarkable wealth of expert talent not only in Germany's staple repertory of Mozart, Wagner and Strauss but also in Italian opera, particularly Verdi who had enjoyed a veritable renaissance starting in Berlin and Dresden in the 1920s.

Literally dozens of singers shine out in every vocal category. Those whose work is catalogued here represent merely a personal selection, whilst others have been included in my previous discographies "Teachers and pupils", "Mezzos and contraltos", "The lyric baritone" and "Six Wagnerian sopranos".

The question which cannot be avoided is why there should have been such a flowering of talent on this exalted level in the German-speaking countries at a time when politics were assuming such a menacing face and whilst suffering and deprivation were affecting millions of lives in the world outside the arts. Some commentators have put forward the argument that the beauty of the performing arts became a refuge from the agonies being endured elsewhere. Others have hinted that the artists concerned (conductors and instrumentalists as well as singers) were simply opportunists using political injustice for their own personal advancement.

Certainly as the twentieth century neared its end a retrospective, and in my view misguided, political correctness began to prevail. It has argued that all prominent figures in the arts world who remained in Nazi Germany, starting at the top with the leading musicians Richard Strauss and Wilhelm Furtwängler, were in some way answerable for, and even complicit in, their country's stance. In contrast it was asserted that colleagues like Fritz Busch, Elisabeth Schumann and Lotte Lehmann, whose chose voluntary exile from their homeland, were paragons of virtue. Even a certain composer long dead before the declaration of the Third Reich is in certain quarters accounted to be responsible for ignominious actions taken by that government. But if William Shakespeare had become Adolf Hitler's idol and not Richard Wagner, would we then declare Shakespeare to be a precursor of National Socialism ?

As far as the opera singers dealt with in this volume are concerned, it has been conveniently overlooked that the tenor Max Lorenz and soprano Maria Müller were already in the 1920s or early 1930s esteemed international performers who travelled professionally beyond Germany. Müller in particular was an established member of the New York Met, singing alongside the likes of Rosa Ponselle, Tito Schipa, Giacomo Lauri-Volpi and Ezio Pinza. The only singer in our German group who seems never to have appeared in America is Franz Völker, and we may never know if that was for personal reasons or if his country's hostile politics prevented it. Helge Rosvaenge arrived belatedly in the USA only in the early 1960s and we possess the living document of his Carnegie Hall recital.

If one wants to encapsulate some of the qualities of these singers, one might sample the scenes from Wagner's *Lohengrin* recorded jointly by Telefunken and Grammophon at Bayreuth in 1936, in which Völker and Müller radiate a rapt enchantment which transcends any thought of mere technique. The several recorded versions by Tiana Lemnitz of Wagner's *Wesendonk-Lieder*, either of her sets of Weber's *Der Freischütz* arias, not to mention *O patria mia!* from Verdi's *Aida*, all reveal the mistress of legato and youthful awe. Described by John Steane as the most comforting of soprano voices, Lemnitz is in fact the true precursor of Elisabeth Grümmer, Elisabeth Schwarzkopf, Lisa della Casa, Gundula Janowitz and Margaret Price. And the vast repertoire of operetta and other popular music and, dare we say it, patriotic material recorded by the tenors Rosvaenge and Völker displays a fluent and beguiling manner which is on a par, in my view even surpasses, the more schmaltzy style of the better known Richard Tauber.

The listener's indebtedness goes out to several pioneers in the record-producing industry. To Walter Legge, who supervised a number of both prewar and postwar sessions for Lemnitz with Electrola/EMI. Even more to the collector Jürgen Grundheber, who in the 1960s and 1970s began to unearth the vast store of *Reichsrundfunk* tapes referred to at the beginning of this introduction. This in turn resulted in the LP publication by BASF/Acanta of an impressive array of double albums devoted to singers of the 1930s and 1940s and of the Michael Raucheisen edition devoted to German song. This, surprisingly, still awaits its reincarnation on CD, but it is heartening that the original LPs are still eagerly sought after in the collector's market. What CD can already offer us is Koch's invaluable compendium of excerpts from Vienna *Staatsoper* performances from precisely that period 1933-1944. It fills countless gaps and reveal insights into the work of these singers in operatic roles which otherwise might have been mere memories in the minds of more senior collectors: Rosvaenge and Lorenz singing Verdi on stage, Völker in his role of Kaiser in Strauss' *Die Frau ohne Schatten*.

The arrangement of the discographical material follows the pattern of previous volumes but with modifications which I hope readers will regard as improvements. Composers' names now appear at the top of *every* page. The first column of data gives precise recording date where known (sadly much information from the Grammophon (Polydor) company will remain imprecise due to the loss of archive material); in the case of operas or operatic excerpts, second column will first name the role assumed by the particular singer, followed by orchestra, chorus, conductor and vocal soloists of the other main roles – if only a single name appears in this second column, it can usually be assumed to be that of a piano accompanist; third column of data lists the catalogue numbers of issues in the main formats of 78, 45, LP and CD (and occasional VHS video). It is in the last area that I am always keen to hear from collectors who might be able to add numbers for rare or overlooked issues.

Lower case usage continues to facilitate reference to the often tightly-packed data, and in this particular volume it can safely be assumed that all the music is sung in German unless otherwise stated – and what is more with impeccable diction. This was standard practice at the time and has absolutely nothing to do with nationalistic feelings or the like !

John Hunt January 2001

helge rosvaenge
1897-1972

STAATS-OPER
UNTER DEN LINDEN

Anfang **20** (8 Uhr)

38. Karten-Reserve-Satz
Außer Abonnement
Oeffentlicher Kartenverkauf

Anfang **20** (8 Uhr)

Die Hugenotten

Oper in 6 Bildern von **Giacomo Meyerbeer**
Nach dem Text von Eugène Scribe für die deutsche Opernbühne völlig neu bearbeitet von Dr. Julius Kapp
Dirigent: General-Musikdirektor Leo Blech
Inszenierung und Choreographie: Gustaf Gründgens a. G.

Raoul de Nangis, protestantischer Edelmann	Helge Roswaenge
Marcel, sein Diener	Emanuel List
Théligny } protestantische Edelleute	Marcel Noë
Damville }	Felix Fleischer-Janczak
Graf von St. Bris, Führer der Katholiken	Walter Großmann
Valentine, seine Tochter	Violetta de Strozzi
Graf von Nevers ⎫	Fritz Krenn
Cossé ⎪	Gustav Rödin
Thoré ⎪	Walter Beck
Tavannes ⎬ katholische Edelleute	Waldemar Henke
Méru ⎪	Martin Abendroth
Maurevert ⎭	Leonhard Kern
Margarete von Valois, die Braut Heinrichs VI. von Navarra	Margherita Perras
Urbain, ihr Page	Tilly de Garmo
Zwei Hofdamen	Else Fink, Margery Booth
Drei Mönche	M. Abendroth, W. Beck, F. Fleischer-Janczak
Stimme des Wächters	Walter Beck
Ein Diener von Nevers	Gerhard Witting

Hofstaat der Königin Margarete / Katholische und protestantische Edelleute
Volk von Paris / Soldaten / Mönche / Geistlichkeit

Die beiden ersten Bilder spielen in der Tourraine, die übrigen in Paris im August 1572

Gesamtausstattung: Rochus Gliese
Bühnentechnische Einrichtung: Rudolf Klein
Dekorationen und Kostüme, hergestellt in den Werkstätten der Staatstheater

Pause nach dem 2. Bilde
Kein Vorspiel

Anfang 20 (8) Uhr   Ende nach 22¾ (10¾) Uhr   Kasseneröffnung 19 (7) Uhr

Gebühr für Kleiderablage: 1. Rang Logen, 1. Rang Balkon, Parkett 0.60 RM, 2. Rang Balkon und Logen 0.40 RM., 3. Rang Balkon und Logen 0.30 RM, 4. Rang Sitzplatz und Stehplatz 0.20 RM.

An der Kasse gekaufte Karten werden nur im Falle der Abänderung einer Vorstellung bis zu deren Beginn gegen Erstattung des Kassenpreises zurückgenommen. Aenderungen in der angekündigten Rollenbesetzung begründen keinen Anspruch auf Preisermäßigung oder auf Rücknahme oder Umtausch der Eintrittskarten.

ADOLPHE ADAM (1803-1856)

le postillon de lonjumeau, excerpt (mes amis écoutez!)
berlin	*role of biju*	78: odeon 0-6588/0-7981
7 february	staatskapelle	78: parlophone P 9210
1928	weissman	cd: pearl GEMMCD 9394
		cd: preiser 89201
		also issued on lp by preiser

berlin	staatskapelle	78: electrola DA 4414
20 may	seidler-winkler	45: electrola E 40040
1936		45: hmv 7P 345
		lp: emi 1C147 29240-29241
		cd: nimbus NI 7899
		cd: preiser 89209/90328
		also issued on lp by preiser

DANIEL AUBER (1782-1871)

fra diavolo, excerpt (pour toujours disait-elle)
berlin	*role of diavolo*	78: electrola DA 4414
20 may	staatskapelle	45: electrola E 40040
1936	seidler-winkler	lp: emi 1C147 29240-29241
		cd: preiser 89209
		also issued on lp by preiser

LUDWIG VAN BEETHOVEN (1770-1827)

fidelio, excerpt (gott welch dunkel hier!/in des lebens frühlingstagen)
berlin	*role of florestan*	78: electrola DB 4522
april	staatskapelle	45: electrola E 41591
1936	seidler-winkler	lp: emi 1C147 29240-29241
		cd: nimbus NI 7899
		cd: grammofono AB 78668-78669
		cd: pearl GEMMCD 9394
		cd: cantus classics CACD 500024
		cd: preiser 89211/90328
		also issued on lp by preiser
vienna	philharmonia	cd: preiser 90103
30 may	hungarica	*also issued on lp by preiser*
1959	rozsnay	
new york	seyfert, piano	lp: preiser PR 3105
1963		

HECTOR BERLIOZ (1803-1869)

la damnation de faust
berlin	berlin radio	unpublished reichsrundfunk broadcast
1943	orchestra	
	staatsoper	
	chorus	
	berger	
	greindl	

GEORGES BIZET (1838-1875)
carmen, abridged opera
berlin	*role of don josé*	78: grammophon 15259-15263/
1930	staatskapelle	27367-27371/95337-95341
	weigert	
	ruziczka	
	marherr	
	domgraf-fassbänder	

carmen, excerpt (la fleur que tu m'avais jetée)
berlin	staatskapelle	78: electrola EH 126
8 february	zweig	cd: preiser 89201
1928		*also issued on lp by preiser*

berlin	staatskapelle	78: electrola DB 4524
april	seidler-winkler	lp: electrola E 83382
1938		lp: emi 1C147 29240-29241
		cd: nimbus NI 7899
		cd: pearl GEMMCD 9394
		cd: cantus classics CACD 500024
		cd: preiser 89211/90328
		also issued on lp by preiser

berlin	berlin radio	lp: acanta KBF 21485
1942	orchestra	lp: historia H 696-697
	rother	

zürich	tonhalle-	78: decca K 2313/K 28174
march	orchester	cd: preiser 90338
1950	reinshagen	

new york	seyfert, piano	lp: preiser PR 3105
1963		

carmen, excerpt (ma mere je la vois)
berlin	staatskapelle	78: grammophon 95451
1931	weigert	45: dg EPL 30 546
	debicka	lp: preiser LV 513
		cd: preiser 89209

carmen, excerpt (c'est toi! c'est moi!)
berlin	unknown	78: grammophon 66818
1928	orchestra and	lp: dg LPE 17 109
	conductor	cd: preiser 89201
	leisner	*also issued on lp by preiser*

CARL BOEHM (1844-1920)

still wie die nacht
berlin	staatskapelle	78: grammophon 24615
1931	melichar	lp: preiser LV 513
	debicka	lp: club 99-17

FRANCOIS BOIELDIEU (1775-1834)

la dame blance, excerpt (viens gentille dame)
berlin	staatskapelle	78: odeon 0-6923
7 february	weissmann	78: parlophone P 9210
1928		cd: pearl GEMMCD 9394
		cd: preiser 89201
		also issued on lp by preiser

HAKON BORRESEN (1876-1954)

hvis du har varme tanker
berlin	seidler-winkler,	78: electrola DA 5224
1940	piano	cd: preiser 89992
	sung in the original danish	

PETER CORNELIUS (1824-1874)

der barbier von bagdad, excerpt (ach das leid hab' ich getragen!)
berlin   *role of nureddin*   78: electrola DA 4465
1939   staatskapelle   lp: emi 1C147 29240-29241
     seidler-winkler   cd: grammofono AB 78668-78669
       cd: cantus classics CACD 500024
       cd: preiser 89211
       also issued on lp by preiser

der barbier von bagdad, excerpt (o holdes bild in engelsschöne)
berlin   staatskapelle   78: electrola DA 4495
1939   seidler-winkler   lp: electrola E 83382
     i.rosvaenge   lp: emi 1C147 29240-29241
       cd: grammofono AB 78668-78669
       cd: preiser 89209
       also issued on lp by preiser

GAETONO DONIZETTI (1797-1848)

l'elisir d'amore, excerpt (una furtiva lagrima)
vienna   *role of nemorino*   electrola unpublished
21 january   vienna
1942   philharmonic
     moralt

lucia di lammermoor, excerpt (chi mi frema in tal momento?)
berlin   *role of edgardo*   lp: acanta KBF 21485
1941   städtische
     oper orchestra
     rother
     piltti
     schilp
     zimmermann
     reinmar
     lang

NICO DOSTAL (1891-1981)

man liebt nur einmal
berlin	paul godwin-	78: grammophon 23147
1930	künstler-	cd: preiser 89225
	orchester	*also issued on lp by preiser*

JENS LAURSEN EMBORG (1876-1957)

agnes mein reizender schmetterling; vollmond am see
berlin	staatskapelle	78: electrola DA 4415
1936	seidler-winkler	cd: preiser 89225
	i.rosvaenge	*also issued on lp by preiser*

LEO FALL (1873-1925)

die geschiedene frau, potpourri
berlin	orchestra	78: grammophon 27250
1931	melichar	lp: preiser LV 514
	claus	cd: preiser 89225

FRIEDRICH VON FLOTOW (1812-1883)

martha, excerpt (ach so fromm)
berlin	*role of lionel*	78: grammophon 10434
25 october	staatskapelle	78: decca DE 7051
1935	martin	45: dg EPL 30 546
		cd: grammofono AB 78868-78869
		cd: dg 459 0072/459 0662
		cd: preiser 89209
		also issued on lp by preiser

martha, excerpt (letzte rose)
berlin	staatskapelle	78: grammophon 10434
25 october	martin	78: decca DE 7051
1935		lp: historia H 696-697
		cd: grammofono AB 78868-78869
		cd: preiser 89209
		also issued on lp by preiser; historia incorrectly dated 1929

martha, excerpt (mag der himmel euch vergeben)
berlin	unknown	78: grammophon 73093
1928	orchestra and	45: dg EPL 30 546
	conductor	lp: preiser LV 511
	debicka	cd: grammofono AB 78868-78869
	leisner	cd: preiser 89201
	watzke	

UMBERTO GIORDANO (1867-1948)

andrea chenier, abridged opera
berlin   *role of chenier*   lp: acanta 10.213617
25 june   berlin radio   cd: preiser 90272
1942   orchestra   *excerpts*
     staatsoper   lp: historia H 696-697
     chorus
     heidersbach
     domgraf-fassbänder
     wrana
     fleischer
     roggen

andrea chenier, excerpt (un di all' azzurro spazio)
new york   seyfert, piano   lp: preiser PR 3105
1963

MIKHAIL GLINKA (1804-1857)

a life for the tsar, excerpt (brothers follow me!)
berlin   *role of sobinin*   78: electrola DB 5563
1940   staatskapelle   45: electrola E 40930
     seidler-winkler   cd: nimbus NI 7899
                                     cd: historia H 696-697
                                     cd: cantus classics CACD 500024
                                     cd: preiser 89211
                                     also issued on lp by preiser

CHARLES GOUNOD (1818-1893)

faust

stuttgart	*role of faust*	lp: ed smith UORC 245
5 december	reichssender	lp: preiser FST 3
1937	orchestra	cd: preiser 90040
	and chorus	cd: arkadia 78056
	keilberth	*excerpts*
	teschemacher	lp: historia H 696-697
	waldenau	cd: myto MCD 94196
	hann	*historia incorrectly names singer of marguérite as*
	nissen	*eipperle in place of teschemacher*
berlin	reichssender	cd: myto MCD 94196/992.H030
6 march	orchestra	
1938	and chorus	
	steiner	
	singestreu	
	arndt-ober	
	bohnen	
	ahlersmayer	

faust, abridged opera

berlin	staatskapelle	78: grammophon 15272-15276/
1930	and chorus	27337-27339/27377-27381/
	weigert	95446-95450
	debicka	
	schulz-dornburg	
	kandl	
	schlusnus	

gounod **faust, excerpt (salut demeure)**

berlin 1928	unknown orchestra and conductor	78: grammophon 66824 45: dg EPL 30 546 cd: preiser 89201 *also issued on lp by preiser*
vienna 10 november 1936	vienna philharmonic krips	lp: ed smith UORC 242 lp: teletheater 762.3589 cd: koch 3-1462-2 *also includes other fragments with helletsgruber, berglund and sved*
berlin april 1939	staatskapelle seidler-winkler	78: electrola DB 4655 45: electrola E 40930 lp: emi 1C147 29240-29241 cd: preiser 89211/90328 *also issued on lp by preiser*
berlin 1942	berlin radio orchestra rother	lp: acanta KBF 21485

faust, excerpt (alerte! alerte!)

berlin 1938	staatskapelle and chorus seidler-winkler teschemacher strienz	78: electrola DB 4507 lp: emi 1C147 29240-29241 cd: cantus classics CACD 500024 cd: preiser 89211 *also issued on lp by preiser*

EDVARD GRIEG (1843-1907)

songs: mit einer primula veris; zwei braune augen; waldwanderung; am schönsten sommerabend
berlin	raucheisen	lp: acanta 10.225054/40.23559
3 june		cd: preiser 89992
1943		

ein schwan
berlin	raucheisen	lp: acanta 10.225054
3 june		cd: preiser 89992
1943		

ein traum
berlin	raucheisen	lp: historia H 696-697
3 june		*incorrectly dated 1936*
1943		

FRANZ GROTHE (1908-1982)

es gab nur eine, die ich geliebt hab'
berlin	paul godwin-	78: grammophon 22986
1930	künstler-	cd: preiser 89225
	orchester	

hajoh! wer fährt mit?
berlin	orchestra	78: grammophon 10422
1935	schwieger	cd: preiser 89225

es ist eine gar alte weise; heute ist für mich die ganze welt zu klein
berlin	orchestra	78: grammophon 10425
1935	schwieger	cd: preiser 89225

songs by grieg and grothe possibly also published on lp by preiser

PETER HEISE (1830-1879)

songs: tornerose/kongesonneus romance; der var en svend med sin pigelil
berlin	seidler-winkler	78: electrola DA 5225
1940	*sung in the*	cd: preiser 89992
	original danish	*also issued on lp by preiser*

aften paa loggiaen
berlin	seidler-winkler	78: electrola DA 5224
1940	*sung in the*	cd: preiser 89992
	original danish	*also issued on lp by preiser*

EMMERICH KALMAN (1882-1953)

das veilchen von montmartre, excerpts (ninon du kind der stadt paris; was weiss ein nie geküsster rosenmund?)
berlin	orchestra	78: grammophon 23631
1930	melichar	lp: preiser LV 514
		cd: preiser 89225

heut' nacht hab' ich geträumt von dir
berlin	ilja-livschakoff	78: grammophon 23638
1930	orchester	cd: preiser 89225
		also issued on lp by preiser

BRONISLAV KAPER (1902-1983)

ein lied aus meiner heimat; schade, dass liebe nur ein märchen ist
berlin   ilja-livschakoff   78: grammophon 24602
1932   orchester   cd: preiser 89225
                                          also issued on lp by preiser

RUDOLF KATTNIGG (1895-1955)

balkanliebe, excerpts (heimatlied und barkarole)
berlin   orchestra   78: electrola EG 6165
1937   seidler-winkler   lp: emi 1C147 29240-29241
                                          cd: preiser 89225
                                          also issued on lp by preiser

der prinz von thule, excerpt (juble mein herz!)
berlin   orchestra   78: electrola EG 6200
1937   seidler-winkler   lp: emi 1C147 29240-29241
                                          cd: preiser 89225
                                          also issued on lp by preiser

HERMANN KROME

übers meer grüss' ich dich, heimatland!
berlin   unknown   78: grammophon 22987
1930   orchestra and   cd: preiser 89225
                     conductor   *also issued on lp by preiser*

EDUARD KUENNEKE (1885-1953)

die grosse sünderin, excerpt (histörchen, geschichten!)
berlin   staatskapelle   78: electrola EG 3519
1935   seidler-winkler   45: electrola E 41478
                                    lp: electrola E 83344/E 83581/HZE 159
                                    lp: emi 1C147 29240-29241
                                    cd: preiser 89209
                                    also issued on lp by preiser

die grosse sünderin, excerpt (das lied vom leben des schrenk)
berlin   staatskapelle   78: electrola EG 3519
1935   seidler-winkler   45: electrola E 41478
                                    lp: electrola E 83581

berlin   staatskapelle   78: grammophon 15099
december   künneke   lp: historia H 696-697
1935   cd: preiser 89209/90328
                                    also issued on lp by preiser

die grosse sünderin, excerpt (immerzu singt dein herz meinem herzen zu)
berlin   staatskapelle   78: electrola EH 947
1935   seidler-winkler   45: electrola E 41478
                                    lp: electrola E 83581

berlin   staatskapelle   78: grammophon 15099
december   künneke   lp: historia H 696-697
1935   lemnitz   lp: club 99-24
                                    lp: acanta 98.221776
                                    lp: preiser LV 516
                                    cd: preiser 89209

die grosse sünderin, excerpt (das lied vom indischen märchen)
berlin   staatskapelle   78: electrola EH 947
1935   seidler-winkler   45: electrola E 41478
                                    lp: emi 1C147 29240-29241
                                    cd: preiser 89209/90328
                                    also issued on lp by preiser

FRANZ LEHAR (1870-1948)

friederike, excerpt (sah ein knab' ein röslein steh'n)
zürich   tonhalle-   78: decca K 2298
12 june   orchester   cd: preiser 90338
1949   reinshagen

der graf von luxemburg, excerpt (bist du's lachendes glück?)
zürich   tonhalle-   78: decca K 2181
1948   orchester   45: decca 45-71134
                 reinshagen   lp: decca LM 4520
                                   lp: london (usa) LS 11
                                   cd: preiser 90338

giuditta, excerpt (freunde das leben ist lebenswert!)
berlin   volksoper   78: electrola DB 7664
1943   orchestra   lp: emi 1C147 29240-29241
                 and chorus   cd: preiser 89211
                 seidler-winkler   *also issued on lp by preiser*

zürich   tonhalle-   78: decca K 2235
1949   orchester   lp: decca LM 4520
                 reinshagen   lp: london (usa) LS 11
                                   cd: preiser 90338

giuditta, excerpt (du bist meine sonne)
berlin   volksoper   78: electrola DB 7664
1943   orchestra   lp: historia H 696-697
                 seidler-winkler   cd: preiser 89211
                                   also issued on lp by preiser

zürich   tonhalle-   78: decca K 2259
1949   orchester   lp: decca LM 4520
                 reinshagen   lp: london (usa) LS 11
                                   cd: preiser 90338

das land des lächelns, excerpt (dein ist mein ganzes herz)
zürich   tonhalle-   78: decca K 2298
12 june   orchester   cd: preiser 90338
1949   reinshagen

new york   seyfert, piano   lp: preiser PR 3105
1963

lehar **die lustige witwe, excerpt (sieh dort den kleinen pavillon)**
zürich   tonhalle-   78: decca K 2235
1949   orchester   lp: decca LM 4520
               reinshagen   lp: london (usa) LS 11
                                  cd: preiser 90338

die lustige witwe, excerpt (da geh' ich zu maxim)
berlin   unknown   78: grammophon 90041
1928   orchestra and   lp: preiser LV 514
               conductor   cd: preiser 89225

die lustige witwe, excerpts (dummer dummer reitersmann!; lippen schweigen)
berlin   unknown   78: grammophon 90042
1928   orchestra and   lp: preiser LV 514
               conductor   cd: preiser 89225
               kochhahn

lehar schön ist die welt , excerpt (schön ist die welt)
berlin	ilja-livschakoff	78: grammophon 23709
1930	orchester	lp: historia H 696-697
		lp: preiser LV 514
		cd: preiser 89225

schön ist die welt, excerpt (liebste glaub' an mich!)
berlin	ilja-livschakoff	78: grammophon 23709
1930	orchester	lp: preiser LV 514
		cd: preiser 89225
zürich	tonhalle-	78: decca K 2259
1949	orchester	lp: decca LM 4520
	reinshagen	lp: london (usa) LS 11
		cd: preiser 90338

der zarewitsch, abridged version for radio
zürich	tonhalle-	78: decca K 23092-23096
1946	orchester	lp: decca LK 4033/BR 3034
	reinshagen	lp: relief RL 826
	della casa	cd: preiser 90338
	funk	*preiser omits the items not involving rosvaenge*
	hendrik	
	jungwirth	

RUGGERO LEONCAVALLO (1858-1919)

i pagliacci

berlin	*role of canio*	lp: dg LPEM 19 247-19 249
1944	berlin radio	cd: preiser 90030
	orchestra*excerpts*	
	and chorus	lp: acanta KBF 21485
	scheppan	*acanta incorrectly describes orchestra as*
	wessely	*staatskapelle*
	hann	
	schmitt-walter	

i pagliacci, excerpt (un tal gioco)

berlin	staatskapelle	78: electrola DA 4472
24 october	seidler-winkler	45: electrola E 40040
1939		lp: emi 1C147 29240-29241
		cd: nimbus NI 7899
		cd: cantus classics CACD 500024
		cd: preiser 89211
		also issued on lp by preiser

i pagliacci, excerpt (vesti la giubba)

berlin	staatskapelle	78: electrola DA 4472
24 october	seidler-winkler	45: electrola E 40040
1939		lp: electrola E 83382
		lp: emi 1C147 29240-29241
		lp: historia H 696-697
		cd: nimbus NI 7899
		cd: preiser 89211/90328
		also issued on lp by preiser
vienna	philharmonia	cd: preiser 90103
30 may	hungarica	*also issued on lp by preiser*
1959	rozsnay	
new york	seyfert, piano	lp: preiser PR 3105
1963		

i pagliacci, excerpt (no pagliaccio non son!)

berlin	staatskapelle	78: electrola DB 5569
30 january	seidler-winkler	lp: electrola E 83382
1940		cd: preiser 89211/90328
		also issued on lp by preiser

PIETRO MASCAGNI (1863-1945)

cavalleria rusticana, excerpt (o lola ch'ai di latti fior di spino)
berlin	*role of turiddu*	78: electrola EH 126
8 february	unknown	cd: preiser 89201
1928	orchestra and conductor	*also issued on lp by preiser*

cavalleria rusticana, excerpt (tu qui santuzza?)
berlin	berlin radio	lp: acanta KBF 21485
1941	orchestra	
	rother	
	scheppan	
	schröder	

cavalleria rusticana, excerpt (no no turiddu rimani!)
vienna	vienna	lp: ed smith EJS 334
26 september	philharmonic	cd: koch 3-1462-2
1933	reichenberger	*also includes other fragments with*
	jeritza	*bokor and schipper*

cavalleria rusticana, excerpt (mamma quel vino e generoso!)
vienna	philharmonia	cd: preiser 90103
30 may	hungarica	*also issued on lp by preiser*
1959	rozsnay	

JULES MASSENET (1842-1912)

manon, excerpt (on l'appelle manon)
berlin	*role of des grieux*	78: grammophon 95452
1929	orchestra	lp: preiser LV 65/LV 513
	gurlitt	lp: historia H 696-697
	debicka	cd: preiser 89201

manon, excerpt (en fermant les yeux)
berlin	staatskapelle	78: electrola DB 4655
1939	seidler-winkler	45: electrola E 40930
		cd: cantus classics CACD 500024
		cd: preiser 89211
		also issued on lp by preiser

manon, excerpt (ah fuyez douce image!)
berlin	berlin	78: telefunken E 2253/SK 1407/TF 154
28 february	philharmonic	lp: telefunken HT 24/642.084J
1933	f.a.schmidt	cd: nimbus NI 7899
		cd: teldec 3984 284102
		cd: preiser 89209
		also issued on lp by preiser

HANS MAY (1886-1958)

ich liebe, du liebst, er liebt
berlin	unknown	78: grammophon 23487
1930	orchestra and	cd: preiser 89225
	conductor	*also issued on lp by preiser*

GIACOMO MEYERBEER (1791-1864)

l'africaine, excerpt (o paradis!)
berlin	*role of vasco*	78: telefunken SK 1407
28 february	berlin	lp: telefunken HT 24
1933	philharmonic	cd: teldec 3894 284102
	f.a.schmidt	cd: preiser 89209
		also issued on lp by preiser

les huguenots, excerpt (plus blanche que la blanche hermine)
berlin	*role of raoul*	78: telefunken SK 1272/TF 22
12 november	staatskapelle	lp: telefunken HT 24
1932	f.a.schmidt	cd: teldec 3894 284102
		cd: preiser 89209
		also issued on lp by preiser

CARL MILLOECKER (1842-1899)

gasparone, excerpt (o dass ich doch der räuber wär'!)
berlin	staatskapelle	78: grammophon 24418
1931	melichar	lp: preiser LV 514
		cd: preiser 89225

der arme jonathan, excerpt (ich bin der arme jonathan)
berlin	staatskapelle	78: grammophon 24418
1931	melichar	lp: preiser LV 514
		cd: preiser 89225

WOLFGANG AMADEUS MOZART (1756-1791)

cosi fan tutte, excerpt (un aura amorosa)
berlin	*role of ferrando*	78: odeon O-6923
7 february	staatskapelle	78: parlophone P 9227
1928	weissman	lp: emi 1C147 29240-29241/EX 29 05983
		cd: pearl GEMMCD 9394
		cd: preiser 89201
		also issued on lp by preiser
vienna	philharmonia	cd: preiser 90103
30 may	hungarica	*also issued on lp by preiser*
1959	rozsnay	

don giovanni, excerpt (dalla sua pace)
berlin	*role of ottavio*	78: odeon O-6588
bruary	staatskapelle	78: parlophone P 9227
1928	weissmann	lp: emi EX 29 05983
		cd: emi CMS 763 7502
		cd: pearl GEMMCD 9394
		cd: preiser 89201
		also issued on lp by preiser
vienna	vienna	electrola unpublished
22 july	philharmonic	
1942	moralt	

mozart don giovanni, excerpt (il mio tesoro)
berlin staatskapelle 78: odeon O-6588/O-7981
7 february weissmann cd: pearl GEMMCD 9394
1928 cd: preiser 89201
also issued on lp by preiser

vienna vienna electrola unpublished
22 july philharmonic
1942 moralt

die entführung aus dem serail, excerpt (hier soll ich dich denn sehen?)
berlin *role of belmonte* 78: electrola DA 4417
1937 staatskapelle 45: electrola E 40930
 seidler-winkler lp: preiser LV 500
 lp: historia H 696-697
 cd: pearl GEMMCD 9129
 cd: grammofono AB 78668-78669
 cd: preiser 89209

die entführung aus dem serail, excerpt (welch ein geschick!)
hamburg ndr orchestra lp: melodram MEL 102
1949 schüchter
 berger

die entführung aus dem serail, excerpts (o wie ängstlich!; wenn der freude tränen fliessen)
vienna vienna electrola unpublished
22 july philharmonic
1942 moralt

mozart **die zauberflöte**

salzburg	*role of tamino*	lp: ed smith DATA 1
30 july	vienna	lp: mrf records MRF 71
1937	philharmonic	lp: toscanini society ATS 1027-1029
	vienna opera	lp: cetra LO 44
	chorus	lp: estro armonico EA 056
	toscanini	cd: melodram MEL 37040
	novotna	cd: grammofono AB 78017-78025/
	osvath	AB 78528-78529
	kipnis	cd: 40s label FTO 321-322
	domgraf-	cd: naxos 811.0828-0829
	fassbänder	*excerpts*
	jerger	lp: historia H 696-697
		lp: amadeo 427 0891
		cd: amadeo 427 0892
		cd: orfeo C394 101B/C408 955R
berlin	berlin	78: hmv DB 3465-3483/
8-15	philharmonic	DB 8475-8493 auto
november	favre chorus	78: electrola C 6371-6389
1937	beecham	78: victor M 541-542
	lemnitz	45: victor WCT 56
	berger	lp: victor LCT 610
	strienz	lp: hmv ALP 1273-1275
	hüsch	lp: electrola E 80471-80473/WCLP 616-618
	grossmann	lp: world records SH 158-160
		lp: angel 6109
		lp: turnabout THS 65078-65080/
		TV 4113-4115
		lp: calig CAL 30845-30846
		lp: emi 143 4653
		cd: emi CHS 761 0342
		cd: nimbus NI 7827-7828
		cd: pearl GEMMCDS 9371
		cd: melodram MEL 27056
		cd: naxos 811.0127-0128
		cd: dutton CDEA 5011
		cd: arkadia 78027
		excerpts
		78: hmv DA 4637
		cd: grammofono AB 78668-78669
		cd: cantus classics CACD 500024
		cd: preiser 89211
		recording completed in february and march 1938; issued in japan both by victor and toshiba

MODEST MUSSORGSKY (1839-1881)

boris godunov, excerpt (dimitri! zarewitsch!)
berlin	*role of dimitri*	78: electrola DB 5593
1943	staatskapelle	cd: cantus classics CACD 500024
	seidler-winkler	cd: preiser 89211
	beckmann	*also issued on lp by preiser*

JACQUES OFFENBACH (1819-1880)

les contes d'hoffman, abridged opera
berlin	*role of hoffman*	78: grammophon 5079-5081/24969-24971
1931	staatskapelle	*excerpts*
	melichar	lp: historia H 696-697
	debicka	
	ruziszka	

les contes d'hoffman, excerpt (c'est une chanson d'amour)
berlin	staatskapelle	78: grammophon 95452/95464
1931	weigert	78: decca CA 8057
	debicka	lp: preiser LV 513
		cd: preiser 89209

les brigands, abridged opera for radio
hamburg	*role of*	lp: ed smith EJS 387
1951	*falsacappa*	*excerpts*
	ndr orchestra	lp: electrola E 83382
	and chorus	
	f.walter	
	freedman	
	minich	
	marschner	
	ahlersmayer	

GIACOMO PUCCINI (1858-1924)

la boheme

stuttgart	*role of rodolfo*	unpublished reichsrundfunk broadcast
5 january	reichssender	
1937	orchestra	
	and chorus	
	spletter	
	callam	
	schmitt-walter	
	hann	
	ducrue	

la boheme, abridged opera

berlin	*role of rodolfo*	78: grammophon 15254-15258/
1930	staatskapelle	27357-27361/95362-95366
	and chorus	
	weigert	
	hüni-mihacsek	
	jungkurth	
	weltner	
	heyer	
	kasenow	

la boheme, excerpt (che gelida manina)

berlin	unknown	78: grammophon 66824/67970
1927	orchestra and	lp: ed smith ANNA 1060
	conductor	cd: pearl GEMMCD 9394
		cd: preiser 89201
		rosvaenge's first recording; also issued on lp by preiser
berlin	berlin radio	lp: acanta KBF 21485/98.221776
9 december	orchestra	lp: historia H 696-697
1941	steinkopf	cd: cantus classics CACD 500024
		cd: preiser 89211/90328
		this recording begins earlier (at chi e la? una donna!) and is a reichsrundfunk recording which was allocated grammophon catalogue numbers 67639-67640

puccini **la boheme, excerpt (o soave fanciulla)**
berlin	orchestra	78: grammophon 66881
1929	gurlitt	lp: preiser LV 65/LV 513
	debicka	cd: preiser 89201/89403
		cd: pearl GEMMCD 9394

berlin	berlin radio	lp: acanta 22.21483-21484
9 december	orchestra	cd: preiser 90248
1941	steinkopf	*reichsrundfunk recording which was allocated*
	cebotari	*grammophon catalogue numbers 67640-67641*

la boheme, excerpt (addio dolce svegliare)
berlin	unknown	78: grammophon 66764
1928	conductor and	cd: preiser 89201
	orchestra	*also issued on lp by preiser*
	hüni-mihacsek	
	de garmo	
	scheidl	

berlin	berlin radio	cd: preiser 90248
9 december	orchestra	*this version begins earlier (at marcello finalmente!)*
1941	steinkopf	*and is a reichsrundfunk recording which was*
	cebotari	*allocated grammophon catalogue numbers*
	schwarzkopf	*67642-67645*
	schmitt-walter	

la boheme, excerpt (o mimi tu piu non torni!)
berlin	staatskapelle	78: electrola DB 4499
october	seidler-winkler	lp: rococo 5375
1937	hüsch	lp: eterna (usa) 721
		cd: pearl GEMMCD 9394
		cd: preiser 89211
		also issued on lp by preiser

la boheme, excerpt (sono andati?)
berlin	orchestra	78: grammophon 66881
1929	gurlitt	lp: preiser LV 65/LV 513
	debicka	cd: preiser 89201
		cd: pearl GEMMCD 9394

puccini **la fanciulla del west, excerpt (ch'ella mi creda)**

vienna	*role of johnson*	cd: preiser 90103
30 may	philharmonia	*also issued on lp by preiser*
1959	hungarica	
	rozsnay	
new york	seyfert, piano	lp: preiser PR 3105
1963		

madama butterfly, excerpt (bimba degli occhi)

berlin	*role of pinkerton*	78: grammophon 66880
1929	orchestra	lp: preiser LV 513
	gurlitt	cd: preiser 89201
	debicka	cd: pearl GEMMCD 9394
berlin	berlin radio	lp: preiser LV 520
1942	orchestra	lp: acanta 22.21483-21484
	rother	cd: preiser 90096
	cebotari	*this version commences at viene la sera*

madama butterfly, excerpt (addio fiorito asil)

berlin	berlin	78: telefunken A 1538
7 june	philharmonic	lp: telefunken HT 24
1933	orthmann	cd: teldec 3984 284102
		cd: pearl GEMMCD 9394
		cd: preiser 89209
		also issued on lp by preiser

tosca

berlin	*role of*	cd: preiser 90210
23 october	*cavaradossi*	cd: cantus classics CACD 500056
1944	berlin radio	*excerpts*
	orchestra	lp: acanta KBF 21485/BB 21497
	and chorus	
	ludwig	
	ranczak	
	hann	

a 1953 performance of tosca in hamburg on ed smith EJS 508 incorrectly ascribed the roles of cavaradossi and tosca to rosvaenge and welitsch respectively: it was later re-issued on eurodisc lp 300 727.420 with the correct attributions of schock and martinis

puccini tosca, excerpt (recondita armonia)

berlin 1927	unknown orchestra and conductor	78: grammophon 66632 45: dg EPL 30 193 cd: preiser 89201 *also issued on lp by preiser*
berlin 1941	berlin radio orchestra steinkopf	lp: acanta 22.221229 cd: preiser 90271
vienna 21 january 1942	vienna philharmonic moralt	78: electrola DA 4504 lp: preiser LV 43/LV 520 cd: preiser 89018/89211/90328 cd: nimbus NI 7899 cd: cantus classics CACD 500024

tosca, excerpt (e lucevan le stelle)

berlin 1927	unknown orchestra and conductor	78: grammophon 66632 45: dg EPL 30 193 cd: preiser 89201 *also issued on lp by preiser*
berlin 1941	berlin radio orchestra steinkopf	lp: acanta 22.221229 cd: preiser 90271
vienna 21 january 1942	vienna philharmonic moralt	78: electrola DA 4504 lp: emi 1C147 29240-29241 lp: preiser LV 43/LV 520 cd: preiser 89018/89211/90328 cd: nimbus NI 7899
berlin 3 march 1957	staatskapelle löwlein	cd: preiser 90103
new york 1963	seyfert, piano	lp: preiser PR 3105

puccini **tosca, excerpt (ah quegli occhi!)**

berlin	staatskapelle	78: electrola DB 4475
may	seidler-winkler	lp: emi 1C147 29240-29241
1937	perras	cd: pearl GEMMCD 9394
		cd: nimbus NI 7899
		cd: preiser 89209
		also issued on lp by preiser

berlin	berlin radio	lp: acanta 22.221229
1941	orchestra	lp: historia H 696-697
	steinkopf	lp: eterna 821 059
	reining	cd: preiser 90271
		this recording begins earlier at perche chiuso?

tosca, excerpt (mario cavaradossi!......to end of opera)

berlin	berlin radio	lp: acanta 22.221229
1941	orchestra	cd: preiser 90096
	steinkopf	*preiser incorrectly names singer of tosca*
	reining	*as ranczak; see also e lucevan le stelle above*

berlin	staatskapelle	cd: preiser 90103
3 march	löwlein	*see also e lucevan le stelle above*
1957	behm	

tosca, excerpt (frascigia a floria tosca!/senti l'ore e vicina)

vienna	vienna	cd: polyhymnia 21212
23 december	philharmonic	
1949	krips	
	welitsch	

puccini **turandot, excerpt (non piangere liu!)**
berlin	*role of calaf*	78: grammophon 10447
1935	staatskapelle	45: dg EPL 30 193
	melichar	lp: dg 2700 708/88 017
		lp: preiser LV 520
		cd: preiser 89209
berlin	berlin radio	cd: preiser 90096
1943	orchestra	
	steinkopf	

turandot, excerpt (nessun dorma)
berlin	staatskapelle	78: grammophon 10447
1935	melichar	45: dg EPL 30 193
		lp: dg 2700 708/88 017
		lp: preiser LV 520
		cd: preiser 89209
berlin	berlin radio	lp: acanta KBF 21485
1943	orchestra	cd: preiser 90096
	and chorus	
	steinkopf	
new york	seyfert, piano	lp: preiser PR 3105
1963		

FRANZ RIES (1846-1932)

wo du hingehst
berlin	staatskapelle	78: grammophon 24615
1931	melichar	lp: preiser LV 513
	debicka	lp: club 99-17

ROBERT STOLZ (1880-1975)

das lied ist aus
berlin	unknown	78: grammophon 23638
1930	orchestra and	cd: preiser 89225
	conductor	*also issued on lp by preiser*

JOHANN STRAUSS (1825-1899)

das lied der liebe, excerpts (du bist mein traum; die eine frau)
berlin	orchestra	78: grammophon 24459
1932	melichar	lp: preiser LV 514
		cd: preiser 89225

die zigeunerbaron, excerpt (wer uns getraut)
berlin	unknown	78: grammophon 95212
1928	orchestra and	lp: preiser LV 514
	conductor	cd: preiser 89225
	kochhahn	

zürich	tonhalle-	78: decca K 2181
1948	orchester	45: decca 45-71134
	reinshagen	lp: decca LM 4520
	della casa	lp: london (usa) LS 11
		cd: preiser 90338

RICHARD STRAUSS (1864-1949)
die ägyptische helena, excerpt (eilig zusammengeraffte gaben!)
vienna	*role of da-ud*	lp: teletheater 120.747
20 september	vienna	cd: koch 3-1455-2
1933	philharmonic	
	vienna opera	
	chorus	
	krauss	
	ursuleac	
	völker	
	jerger	

ariadne auf naxos, version without vorspiel
berlin	*role of bacchus*	lp: ed smith EJS 300
11 june	reichssender	lp: acanta 22.214903/KBF 21806
1935	orchestra	cd: arlecchino ARL 14-16
	krauss	cd: preiser 90259
	ursuleac	*22.214903 incorrectly stated that recording*
	berger	*took place in stuttgart*
	hammes	

der rosenkavalier
salzburg	*role of sänger*	lp: cetra LO 69
12 august	vienna	cd: arlecchino ARL 46-48
1949	philharmonic	*excerpts*
	vienna opera	lp: gioielli della musica GML 45
	chorus	
	reining	
	güden	
	novotna	
	hann	
	prohaska	

der rosenkavalier, excerpt (di rigori armato)
berlin	staatskapelle	78: electrola DA 4465
18 november	seidler-winkler	45: hmv 7P 345
1938		lp: electrola E 83382
		cd: preiser 89211/89999/90328
		also issued on lp by preiser

berlin	berlin radio	lp: acanta 98.221776/KBF 21485
1942	orchestra	lp: historia H 696-697
	steinkopf	

vienna	philharmonia	cd: preiser 90103
30 may	hungarica	*also issued on lp by preiser*
1959	rozsnay	

new york	seyfert, piano	lp: preiser PR 3105
1963		

strauss ach lieb ich muss nun scheiden/schlichte weisen
berlin	seidler-winkler,	78: electrola DA 4412
1936	piano	cd: preiser 89992
		also issued on lp by preiser

freundliche vision (nicht im schlafe hab' ich das geträumt)
berlin	seidler-winkler,	78: electrola DA 4412
1936	piano	cd: preiser 89992
		also issued on lp by preiser

zueignung (ja du weisst es teure seele!)
vienna	philharmonia	cd: preiser 90103
30 may	hungarica	*also issued on lp by preiser*
1959	rozsnay	
new york	seyfert, piano	lp: preiser PR 3105
1963		

PIOTR TCHAIKOVSKY (1840-1893)

the enchantress, excerpt (my fate is strange)
berlin	*role of yuri*	78: electrola DB 5624
1941	staatskapelle	lp: rococo 5203
	baltzer	lp: eterna (usa) 736
	lemnitz	lp: preiser LV 43/LV 519
		lp: historia H 704-705
		lp: world records SHB 47
		cd: preiser 89211
		cd: hamburger archiv für gesangskunst HAGLEM 2
		cd: cantus classics CACD 500024

evgeny onegin, excerpt (faint echo of my youth)
berlin	*role of lenski*	78: electrola DB 5580
1940	staatskapelle	cd: nimbus NI 7899
	seidler-winkler	cd: cantus classics CACD 500024
		cd: preiser 89211
		also issued on lp by preiser

AMBROISE THOMAS (1811-1896)

mignon, excerpt (froh und frei will ich eilen)
berlin	*role of wilhelm*	78: grammophon 10422
1935	staatskapelle	cd: preiser 89209
	martin	*also issued on lp by preiser*

GIUSEPPE VERDI (1813-1901)

aida

stuttgart	*role of radames*	cd: preiser 90274
24 april	reichssender	*excerpts*
1938	orchestra	lp: acanta 77.221792/KBF 21485/
	and chorus	DE 23057
	keilberth	lp: historia H 696-697
	teschemacher	cd: preiser 90068
	karen	
	hann	
	weber	

hamburg	ndr orchestra	lp: cetra opera live
1951	and chorus	
	schmidt-isserstedt	
	zadek	
	höngen	
	metternich	
	fehn	

aida, excerpt (pur ti riveggo!)

berlin	unknown	78: grammophon 66766
1928	orchestra and	cd: grammofono AB 78668-78669
	conductor	cd: preiser 89201
	hüni-mihacsek	*also issued on lp by preiser*

verdi aida, excerpt (celeste aida)

berlin	berlin	78: telefunken SK 1427
19 june	philharmonic	lp: telefunken HT 24
1933	orthmann	cd: teldec 3984 284102
		cd: preiser 89209
		also issued on lp by preiser

berlin	staatskapelle	78: electrola DB 5580
17 june	seidler-winkler	lp: electrola E 83382/C 91297
1940		lp: emi 1C147 29240-29241/EX 29 10753
		lp: preiser LV 520
		cd: preiser 89211/90068/90328
		cd: grammofono AB 78668-78669
		cd: cantus classics CACD 500024

berlin	berlin radio	lp: acanta KBF 21485
1942	orchestra	cd: preiser 90096
	rother	

zürich	tonhalle-	78: decca K 2313
march	orchester	cd: preiser 90338
1950	reinshagen	

aida, excerpt (gia i sacerdoti adunansi!)

berlin	unknown	78: grammophon 66819
1929	orchestra and	cd: preiser 89201
	conductor	*also issued on lp by preiser*
	leisner	

berlin	staatskapelle	78: electrola DB 7720
1943	seidler-winkler	lp: preiser LV 520
	beckmann	cd: grammofono AB 78668-78669
		cd: preiser 89211/90068
		. *this version commences at l'abborrita rivale!*

aida, excerpt (la fatal pietra)

berlin	unknown	78: grammophon 66767
1928	orchestra and	lp: dg LPE 17 109
	conductor	cd: grammofono AB 78668-78669
	hüni-mihacsek	cd: preiser 89201
		also issued on lp by preiser

48
verdi **un ballo in maschera**

berlin	*role of riccardo*	cd: eklipse EKR 30
1943	berlin radio	*excerpts*
	orchestra	lp: acanta KBF 21485
	städtische oper	lp: historia H 696-697
	chorus	cd: preiser 90096/90273
	rother	cd: cantus classics CACD 500024
	scheppan	
	schilp	
	reichelt	
	schmitt-walter	

un ballo in maschera, excerpt (di tu se fedele)

berlin	staatskapelle	78: electrola D 4445/DB 4646
17 march	and chorus	78: victor 17560
1936	seidler-winkler	lp: electrola E 83382
		lp: emi 1C147 29240-29241
		cd: grammofono AB 78668-78669
		cd: preiser 89209/90328
		also issued on lp by preiser

vienna	volksoper	lp: decca LX 3126
1953	orchestra	
	and chorus	
	loibner	

un ballo in maschera, excerpt (la rivedra nell' estasi)

vienna	volksoper	lp: decca LX 3126
1953	orchestra	
	loibner	

verdi un ballo in maschera, excerpt (teco io sto)
vienna	volksoper	lp: decca LX 3126
1953	orchestra	
	loibner	
	martinis	

un ballo in maschera, excerpt (ma se m'e forza perderti)
berlin	staatskapelle	78: grammophon 67211
11 november	f.a.schmidt	45: dg EPL 30 547
1935		cd: grammofono AB 78668-78669
		cd: preiser 89209
		also issued on lp by preiser

vienna	volksoper	lp: decca LX 3126
1953	orchestra	
	loibner	

don carlo, excerpt (e lui! desso! l'infante!)
berlin	*role of carlo*	lp: acanta KBF 21487/DE 21487
1941	berlin radio	lp: historia H 696-697
	orchestra	cd: cantus classics CACD 500024/
	rother	CACD 500028
	schlusnus	

la forza del destino, excerpt (o tu che in seno agli angeli)
berlin	*role of alvaro*	78: grammophon 67211
11 november	staatskapelle	45: dg EPL 30 547
1935	f.s.schmidt	cd: dg 459 0052/459 0662
		cd: grammofono AB 78668-78669
		cd: preiser 89209
		also issued on lp by preiser

berlin	berlin radio	lp: historia H 696-697
1942	orchestra	cd: cantus classics CACD 500024/
	rother	CACD 500028

vienna	philharmonia	cd: preiser 90103
30 may	hungarica	*also issued on lp by preiser*
1959	rozsnay	

verdi **la forza del destino, excerpt (solenne in quest' ora)**

berlin	staatskapelle	78: electrola DB 4499
october	seidler-winkler	lp: rococo 5247
1937	hüsch	cd: pearl GEMMCD 9394
		cd: grammofono AB 78668-78669
		cd: preiser 89211
		also issued on lp by preiser

berlin	berlin radio	lp: acanta BB 23.119
1942	orchestra	cd: myto MCD 93279
	rother	
	schlusnus	

la forza del destino, excerpt (ne gustare m'e dalo)

berlin	berlin radio	cd: myto MCD 93279
1942	orchestra	
	rother	
	schlusnus	

otello, excerpt (niun mi tema)

berlin	*role of otello*	78: telefunken SK 1427
19 june	berlin	lp: telefunken HT 24
1933	philharmonic	cd: teldec 3984 284102
	orthmann	cd: preiser 89209
		also issued on lp by preiser

berlin	staatskapelle	cd: preiser 90271
1943	steinkopf	cd: cantus classics CACD 500024
		cantus classics names conductor as elmendorff

verdi otello, excerpt (gia nella notte densa)
berlin	staatskapelle	lp: acanta 22.22122
1943	steinkopf	lp: eterna 821 059
	reining	cd: preiser 90271
		acanta names conductor as elmendorff

otello, excerpt (desdemona rea!/Si per ciel!)
berlin	staatskapelle	lp: historia H 696-697
1943	steinkopf	cd: preiser 90271
	reinmar	*historia contains si per ciel only*

rigoletto
berlin	*role of duke*	lp: urania URLP 222
20-22	staatskapelle	lp: dg LPEM 19 222-19 223/
november	and chorus	88 026-88 027
1944	heger	lp: eterna 820 152-820 153
	berger	cd: preiser 90036
	klose	*excerpts*
	schlusnus	lp: historia H 696-697
	greindl	

rigoletto, excerpt (questa o quella)
berlin	unknown	78: grammophon 62660
1928	orchestra and	cd: grammofono AB 78668-78669
	conductor	cd: preiser 89201
		also issued on lp by preiser

berlin	staatskapelle	cd: preiser 90272
19 march	and chorus	*also includes preceding scene with borsa*
1942	rother	
	kurz	

verdi **rigoletto, excerpt (e il sol dell' anima)**

berlin	staatskapelle	78: electrola DB 4445
march	seidler-winkler	lp: electrola E 83382
1936	korjus	lp: emi 1C147 29240-29241/
		1C147 30819-30820
		cd: preiser 89209
		also issued on lp by preiser

berlin	staatskapelle	45: dg EPL 30 532
19 march	rother	lp: acanta 22.21483-21484
1942	cebotari	lp: melodiya M10 40957-40958
	waldenau	lp: historia H 677-678
	domgraf-	lp: dg LPEM 19 348
	fassbänder	cd: cantus classics CACD 500024
		cd: preiser 90160/90272
		dg and preiser issues including preceding scene giovanna ho dei rimorsi!

rigoletto, excerpt (parmi veder le lagrime)

vienna	vienna	electrola unpublished
21 january	philharmonic	
1942	moralt	

rigoletto, excerpt (la donna e mobile!)

berlin	unknown	78: grammophon 62660
1928	orchestra and	45: dg EPL 30 547
	conductor	cd: grammofono AB 78668-78669
		cd: preiser 89201
		also issued on lp by preiser

berlin	staatskapelle	cd: preiser 90272
19 march	rother	*also includes preceding scene e l'ami?*
1942	cebotari	
	domgraf-fassbänder	
	kurz	

verdi rigoletto, excerpt (bella figlia dell' amore!)

berlin	unknown	78: grammophon 66765/67363
1928	orchestra and	lp: dg LPEM 19 348
	conductor	cd: grammofono AB 78668-78669
	hüni-mihacsek	cd: preiser 89201
	leisner	*also issued on lp by preiser*
	scheidl	

berlin	staatskapelle	78: telefunken SK 1162
june	meyrowitz	lp: telefunken HT 24/642.084J
1932	yoder	lp: preiser LV 515
	kindermann	cd: preiser 89209
	reinmar	

berlin	staatskapelle	lp: acanta 22.21383-21384/DE 22695
19 march	rother	cd: preiser 90272
1942	cebotari	
	waldenau	
	domgraf-fassbänder	

la traviata, excerpt (un di felice)

berlin	*role of alfredo*	78: electrola DB 4458
1936	staatskapelle	lp: electrola E 83382
	seidler-winkler	lp: historia H 696-697
	perras	cd: grammofono AB 78668-78669
		cd: preiser 89209
		also issued on lp by preiser

berlin	staatskapelle	lp: urania URLP 7011
12-15	and chorus	lp: acanta 10.214982/BB 21498/
january	steinkopf	22.21483-21484
1942	cebotari	lp: elite special PLPS 30071
		lp: austrophon SOLP 30071
		lp: musical heritage MHS 7029
		lp: saga FID 2104
		cd: preiser 90160
		includes preceding chorus libiamo ne' lieti calici!
		and following recitative amor dunque non piu

verdi **la traviata, excerpt (sempre libera!)**

berlin	staatskapelle	lp: urania URLP 7011
12-15	steinkopf	lp: acanta 10.214982/BB 21498
january	cebotari	lp: elite special PLPS 30071
1942		lp: austrophon SOLP 30071
		lp: musical heritage MHS 7029
		lp: saga FID 2104
		lp: historia H 677-678
		cd: preiser 90160

la traviata, excerpt (de' miei bollenti spriti)

berlin	staatskapelle	78: electrola EG 814
8 february	zweig	cd: preiser 89201
1928		*also issued on lp by preiser*

berlin	berlin	78: telefunken A 1538
7 june	philharmonic	lp: telefunken HT 24
1933	orthmann	cd: teldec 3984 269192/3984 284102
		cd: grammofono AB 78668-78669
		cd: preiser 89201
		also issued on lp by preiser

berlin	staatskapelle	78: electrola DB 4646/DB 4495
8 february	seidler-winkler	lp: historia H 696-697
1937		cd: nimbus NI 7848
		cd: preiser 89209/90328
		also issued on lp by preiser

berlin	staatskapelle	lp: urania URLP 7011
12-15	steinkopf	lp: acanta 22.21483-21484
january		lp: elite special PLPS 30071
1942		lp: austrophon SOLP 30071
		lp: musical heritage MHS 7029
		lp: saga FID 2104
		cd: preiser 90160

verdi la traviata, excerpt (che fai? nulla! scrivevi?)
berlin	staatskapelle	lp: urania URLP 7011
12-15	steinkopf	lp: acanta 22.21483-21485/BB 21498/
january	cebotari	KBF 21485
1942		lp: saga FID 2104/FID 2143
		lp: emi EX 29 10753
		cd: preiser 90160
		KBF 21485 incorrectly describes conductor as heger

la traviata, excerpt (invitato a qui seguirmi/di sprezzo degno se stesso rende!... to end of act two)
berlin	staatskapelle	cd: preiser 90160
12-15	and chorus	
january	steinkopf	
1942	cebotari	
	schlusnus	

la traviata, excerpt (parigi o cara!)
berlin	staatskapelle	78: electrola DB 4458
1936	seidler-winkler	cd: preiser 89209
	perras	*also issued on lp by preiser*

berlin	staatskapelle	45: dg EPL 30 536
12-15	steinkopf	lp: urania URLP 7011
january	cebotari	lp: acanta 22.21483-21484/10.214982/
1942		BB 21498
		lp: saga FID 2104
		cd: cantus classics CACD 500024
		cd: preiser 90160

il trovatore
stuttgart	*role of manrico*	cd: preiser 90382
18 october	reichssender	
1936	orchestra	
	and chorus	
	zimmermann	
	reining	
	karen	
	nissen	
	strienz	

verdi **il trovatore, excerpt (ah si ben mio!)**

berlin 23 may 1927	staatskapelle viebig	78: electrola EG 814 cd: preiser 89201 *also issued on lp by preiser*
berlin april 1938	staatskapelle seidler-winkler	78: electrola DB 4524 lp: electrola E 83382 lp: emi 1C147 29240-29241 cd: nimbus NI 7899 cd: pearl GEMMCD 9394 cd: grammofono AB 78668-78669 cd: preiser 89211/90328 *also issued on lp by preiser*
berlin 1942	berlin radio orchestra rother	lp: acanta KBF 21485
vienna 30 may 1959	philharmonia hungarica rozsnay	cd: preiser 90103 *also issued on lp by preiser*
new york 1963	seyfert, piano	lp: preiser PR 3105

verdi il trovatore, excerpt (di quella pira!)

berlin 1928	unknown orchestra and conductor	78: grammophon 67104/73092 45: dg EPL 30 547 cd: preiser 89201 *also issued on lp by preiser*
berlin april 1938	staatskapelle seidler-winkler	78: electrola DB 4524 lp: electrola E 83382 lp: emi 1C147 29240-29241/EX 29 01313 lp: angel IC-6140 cd: nimbus NI 7899 cd: grammofono AB 78668-78669 cd: pearl GEMMCD 9394 cd: preiser 90328 *also issued on lp by preiser*
berlin 1942	berlin radio orchestra rother	lp: historia H 696-697 lp: acanta KBF 21485 cd: preiser 90096
vienna 30 may 1959	philharmonia hungarica rozsnay	cd: preiser 90103 *also issued on lp by preiser*
new york 1963	seyfert, piano	lp: preiser PR 3105

il trovatore, excerpt (di geloso amor sprezzato)

berlin 1928	unknown orchestra and conductor hüni-mihacsek scheidl	78: grammophon 66765/67363 cd: preiser 89201 *also issued on lp by preiser*
vienna 30 april 1951	vienna philharmonic rossi welitsch baylé	cd: polyhymnia 21212 *this extract continues to the end of act one*

verdi il trovatore, excerpt (non son tuo figlio!)

berlin	berlin radio	cd: preiser 90273
26-27	orchestra	cd: cantus classics CACD 500024/CACD 5002
may	rother	*cantus classics version begins later at mal reggendo*
1942	schilp	*all' aspro assalte*

il trovatore, excerpt (quel suon quelle preci!)

berlin	unknown	78: grammophon 67104/73093
1928	orchestra and	lp: preiser LV 511
	conductor	cd: preiser 89201
	debicka	

il trovatore, excerpt (madre non dormi?)

berlin	berlin radio	lp: acanta KBF 21485
26-27	orchestra	cd: preiser 90273
may	rother	*this extract continues to the end of the opera;*
1942	scheppan	*KBF 21485 begans later after entrance of luna*
	schilp	
	schmitt-walter	
	dörr	

berlin	staatskapelle	lp: preiser LV 520
1943	seidler-winkler	cd: preiser 89211
	beckmann	cd: cantus classics CACD 500028
		unpublished electrola 78rpm recording

i vespri siciliani

frankfurt	*role of arrigo*	cd: myto MCD 93279
1951	hessischer	*excerpts*
	rundfunk	lp: dg LPE 17 109/LPEM 19 137
	orchestra	
	and chorus	
	schröder	
	cunitz	
	schlusnus	
	von rohr	

excerpts from il trovatore recorded on 26-27 may 1942 are from a reichsrundfunk broadcast which may survive complete

verdi i vespri siciliani, excerpt (giorno di pianto!)
berlin	staatskapelle	78: telefunken SK 1272
12 november	f.a.schmidt	lp: telefunken HT 11/HT 24/HT 31/HTK 30
1932		lp: emi EX 29 10753
		cd: teldec 3984 284102
		cd: grammofono AB 78668-78669
		cd: preiser 89209
		cd: symposium 1280
		also issued on lp by preiser; emi issue is incorrectly dated 1944

i vespri siciliani, excerpt (sogno o son desto?)
berlin	staatskapelle	78: grammophon 90204
1933	schüler	cd: preiser 89209
	schlusnus	cd: symposium 1280
		also issued on lp by preiser, who name conductor as melichar
berlin	berlin radio	cd: preiser 90096
1942	orchestra	cd: cantus classics CACD 500028
	rother	
	schlusnus	

messa da requiem
london	bbc so and	lp: ed smith UORC 108/MKR 1001-1002
27 may	choral society	lp: toscanini society ATS 1108-1109
1938	toscanini	cd: melodram MEL 28022
	milanov	
	thorborg	
	moscona	
stuttgart	reichssender	lp: discophilia K 18-19
8 november	orchestra	lp: preiser LV 151-152
1938	karlsruhe	cd: preiser 90068
	chorus	
	keilberth	
	teschemacher	
	willer	
	hann	
salzburg	vienna	lp: cetra LO 524
14 august	philharmonic	lp: discocorp RR 391
1949	wiener	lp: rodolphe RP 12403-12404
	singverein	lp: dei della musica DMV 34-35
	karajan	cd: datum DAT 12323
	zadek	cd: preiser 90445
	klose	
	christoff	

RICHARD WAGNER (1813-1883)

lohengrin, excerpt (in fernem land)

vienna	*role of lohengrin*	78: electrola DB 5698
21 january	vienna	lp: emi RLS 7711/1C137 54390-54396M
1942	philharmonic	lp: preiser LV 43/LV 518
	moralt	cd: preiser 89211
		cd: nimbus NI 7899
		cd: grammofono AB 78668-78669
		cd: cantus classics CACD 500024
		cantus classics incorrectly describe orchestra and conductor as staatskapelle and seidler-winkler

new york	seyfert, piano	lp: preiser PR 3105
1963		

lohengrin, excerpt (mein lieber schwan)

vienna	vienna	78: electrola DB 5698
21 january	philharmonic	lp: emi RLS 7711/1C137 54390-54396M/
1942	moralt	1C181 30669-30678M/EX 29 02123
		lp: preiser LV 43/LV 518
		cd: preiser 89211
		cd: emi CMS 764 0082
		cd: nimbus NI 7899
		cd: grammofono AB 78668-78669

wagner die meistersinger von nürnberg, excerpt (am stillen herd)

berlin	*role of stolzing*	78: telefunken SK 1297/SK 2090
24 november	staatskapelle	78: ultraphon G 22604
1932	f.a.schmidt	lp: telefunken HT 11/HT 24
		cd: nimbus NI 7899
		cd: grammofono AB 78668-78669
		cd: teldec 3984 269192/3984 284102
		cd: preiser 89209
		also issued on lp by preiser; teldec issue is dated 14 november 1932

die meistersinger von nürnberg, excerpt (morgenlich leuchtend)

berlin	staatskapelle	78: telefunken SK 1297
24 november	f.a.schmidt	78: ultraphon G 22604
1932		78: mercury DMS 37
		lp: telefunken HT 11/HT 24
		cd: nimbus NI 7899
		cd: grammofono AB 78668-78669
		cd: teldec 3984 284102
		cd: preiser 89209
		also issued on lp by preiser; teldec issue is dated 14 november 1932

die meistersinger von nürnberg, excerpt (selig wie die sonne)

berlin	staatskapelle	78: telefunken SK 1162
june	meyrowitz	lp: telefunken HT 12/HT 24/642.084J
1932	yoder	lp: top classics TC 9042
	kindermann	lp: preiser LV 515
	kuttner	cd: preiser 89209
	reinmar	cd: grammofono AB 78668-78669

CARL MARIA VON WEBER (1786-1826)

der freischütz, excerpt (länger trag' ich nicht die qualen/durch die wälder)
berlin   *role of max*   78: electrola DA 4418
september   staatskapelle   lp: historia H 696-697
1936   seidler-winkler   cd: grammofono AB 78668-78669
                                     cd: pearl GEMMCD 9394
                                     cd: preiser 89209
                                     also issued on lp by preiser

oberon
berlin   *role of huon*   cd: koch 3-1646-2
15 august   reichssender
1938   orchestra
          and chorus
          rosbaud
          teschemacher
          schilp
          holmdonner
          w.ludwig
          schmitt-walter

oberon, excerpt (von jugend auf im kampfgefilde)
berlin   staatskapelle   78: electrola DA 4416
september   seidler-winkler   lp: emi 1C147 29240-29241
1936   cd: nimbus NI 7899
                                     cd: grammofono AB 78668-78669
                                     cd: preiser 89018/89209/89229/90328
                                     also issued on lp by preiser

berlin   berlin radio   lp: acanta KBF 21485
1942   orchestra
          heger

vienna   philharmonia   cd: preiser 90103
30 may   hungarica   *also issued on lp by preiser*
1959   rozsnay

oberon, excerpt (vater hör' mein flehen!)
berlin   staatskapelle   78: electrola DA 4417
september   seidler-winkler   lp: electrola E 83382
1936   cd: preiser 89209
                                     also issued on lp by preiser

KURT WEILL (1900-1950)

die dreigroschenoper, version without dialogue
vienna	*role of ausrufer*	lp: vanguard VRS 9002
1953-1954	instrumental	lp: amadeo AVRS 6023
	ensemble	cd: amadeo 423 8102
	vienna opera	
	chorus	
	adler	
	felbermayer	
	fassler	
	anday	
	jerger	
	preger	
	guthrie	

RUDOLF WILLE

die königsballade, excerpts (euren könig will ich preisen; ewig muss ich dein gedenken)
berlin	staatskapelle	78: electrola DB 4623
18 november	seidler-winkler	lp: electrola E 83382
1938		cd: preiser 89211/90328
		also issued on lp by preiser

küss' die hand, schöne frau!
berlin	staatskapelle	78: electrola EG 6200
1937	seidler-winkler	cd: preiser 89225

HUGO WOLF (1860-1903)

denk' es o seele!/mörike-lieder
berlin   raucheisen   lp: acanta 10.225054
1943   cd: preiser 89992

erwartung/eichendorff-lieder
berlin   raucheisen   lp: acanta 10.225054/23.580
9 february   cd: preiser 89992
1943

der feuerreiter/mörike-lieder
berlin   moore   78: electrola DB 3321
29 august   lp: emi RLS 759/1C163 03991-03997M
1937   lp: historia H 696-697
                                      cd: emi CHS 566 6402
                                      cd: pearl GEMMCDS 9085
                                      cd: preiser 89992
                                      also issued on lp by preiser

berlin   raucheisen   lp: acanta 10.225054/23.580
27 october   cd: preiser 89992
1943

gesellenlied (kein meister fällt vom himmel!)
berlin   moore   78: electrola DB 3321
29 august   lp: emi RLS 759/1C163 03991-03997M
1937   cd: emi CHS 566 6402
                                      cd: pearl GEMMCDS 9085
                                      cd: preiser 89992
                                      also issued on lp by preiser

berlin   raucheisen   lp: acanta 10.225054
1943   cd: preiser 89992

wolf **heimweh/eichendorff-lieder**
berlin   raucheisen   lp: acanta 10.225054/23.580
9 february   cd: preiser 89992
1943

im frühling/mörike-lieder
berlin   raucheisen   lp: acanta 10.225054/23.580
1943   cd: preiser 89992

lieber alles/eichendorff-lieder
berlin   raucheisen   lp: acanta 10.225054
1943   cd: preiser 89992

morgenstimmung (bald ist der nacht ein end' gemacht)
berlin   raucheisen   lp: acanta 10.225054
1943   cd: preiser 89992

der musikant/eichendorff-lieder
berlin   raucheisen   lp: acanta 10.225054
1943   cd: preiser 89992

seemanns abschied/eichendorff-lieder
berlin   raucheisen   lp: acanta 10.225054
1943   cd: preiser 89992

verschwiegene liebe/eichendorff-lieder
berlin   raucheisen   lp: acanta 10.225054
1943   cd: preiser 89992

der verzweifelte liebhaber/eichendorff-lieder
berlin   raucheisen   lp: acanta 10.225054/23.580
9 february
1943

CARL ZELLER (1842-1898)

der obersteiger, potpourri
berlin	orchestra	78: grammophon 27195
1930	and chorus	lp: preiser LV 514
	melichar	cd: preiser 89225
	kochhahn	

MISCELLANEOUS

helge rosvaenge erzählt aus seinem leben
rosvaenge speaks in german about his life and career	lp: preiser PR 3126

MISCELLANEOUS POPULAR SONGS

aus meiner jugend
berlin staatskapelle 78: electrola EG 3693
1936 seidler-winkler cd: preiser 89225

deine mutter bleibt immer bei dir
berlin unknown 78: grammophon 22987
1930 orchestra and cd: preiser 89225
 conductor

du blonde lindenwirtin vom rhein
berlin unknown 78: grammophon 23630
1930 orchestra and cd: preiser 89225
 conductor

du hast mich nie geliebt
berlin paul godwin- 78: grammophon 23147
1930 künstler- cd: preiser 89225
 orchester

immer nur ran
berlin unknown 78: grammophon 24654
1932 orchestra and cd: preiser 89225
 conductor

mein herz hat dich so viel zu fragen
berlin staatskapelle 78: electrola EG 3693
1936 seidler-winkler cd: preiser 89225

mein herz hat leise dein herz gegrüsst
berlin unknown 78: grammophon
1930 orchestra and cd: preiser 89225
 conductor

miscellaneous popular songs/concluded

oh fräulein grete!
berlin	ilja livschakoff-	78: grammophon 23612
1930	orchester	cd: preiser 89225

santa lucia
berlin	unknown	78: grammophon 24654
1932	orchestra and	cd: preiser 89225
	conductor	
	sung in the	
	original italian	

schenk' mir eine tafel schokolade
berlin	ilja-livschakoff-	78: grammophon 23612
1930	orchester	cd: preiser 89225

zwei rote lippen und ein roter tarragona
berlin	paul godwin-	78: grammophon 22986
1930	künstler-	cd: preiser 89225
	orchester	

Opernmusik

auf
ELECTROLA
und
COLUMBIA
Musikplatten

tiana lemnitz
1897-1994

JOHANN SEBASTIAN BACH (1685-1750)

matthäus-passion
leipzig	gewandhaus-	78: electrola DB 7625-7640
march	orchester	78: hmv DB 6516-6531/
1941	thomanerchor	DB 9165-9180auto
	ramin	lp: electrola E 83020-83022/
	beckmann	WCLP 588-590
	erb	lp: eterna 820 625-820 627
	schulze	lp: emi 1C147 29191-29193/
	hüsch	EX 29 12203
		lp: calig CAL 30859-30860
		cd: calig CAL 50859-50860
		cd: preiser 90228

excerpts
lp: electrola E 91271
soprano arias recorded by lemnitz on 27 march

ave maria, arranged by gounod
berlin	städtische oper	78: telefunken A 11153/A099T
11 may	orchestra	lp: telefunken UV 228
1953	lutze	lp: telefunken (canada) GF 63018

LUDWIG VAN BEETHOVEN (1770-1827)

klärchen-lieder/egmont: die trommel gerühret; freudvoll und leidvoll
berlin	berlin radio	lp: rococo 5363
24 august	orchestra	cd: hamburger archiv für gesangskunst
1944	rother	HAGLEM 1

*rococo incorrectly states that lieder are
accompanied by raucheisen at the piano;
HAGLEM 1 gives recording date as 28 february 1944*

JOHANNES BRAHMS (1833-1897)

feldeinsamkeit (ich ruhe still im hohen grünen gras)
berlin   klust   lp: world records SHB 47
18 february   cd: emi CZS 569 7432
1948   *unpublished electrola 78rpm recording*

berlin   ramin   lp: rococo 5320
7 april   *recorded at the singer's farewell recital*
1957

heimweh II (o wüsst' ich doch den weg zurück)
berlin   ramin   lp: rococo 5320
7 april   *recorded at the singer's farewell recital*
1957

immer leiser wird mein schlummer
berlin   raucheisen   78: electrola DB 5540
1939   lp: rococo 5273
           lp: preiser LV 126
           lp: club 99-24
           lp: historia H 704-705
           cd: preiser 89115
           historia incorrectly dated 1940

von ewiger liebe (dunkel wie dunkel in wald und in feld)
berlin   raucheisen   78: electrola DB 5540
1939   lp: rococo 5273
           lp: preiser LV 126
           cd: preiser 89115

berlin   ramin   lp: rococo 5320
7 april   *recorded at the singer's farewell recital*
1957

wiegenlied (guten abend gut' nacht)
berlin   klust   78: electrola DA 5506
18 february   lp: world records SHB 47
1948

PETER CORNELIUS (1824-1874)

hirschlein ging im wald spazieren
berlin   raucheisen   lp: urania URLP 7013
4 may   lp: classics club X 153
1943   lp: acanta 40.23503
                                    cd: melodram MEL 27050

ich und du, duet
berlin   raucheisen   lp: classics club X 153
16 november   schmitt-walter   lp: acanta 40.23503
1944

im lenz wenn veilchen blüh'n
berlin   raucheisen   lp: urania URLP 7013
4 may   lp: classics club X 153
1943   lp: acanta 40.23503

komm' wir wandeln zusammen
berlin   raucheisen   lp: urania URLP 7013
4 may   lp: acanta 40.23503
1943   cd: melodram MEL 27050

möcht' im walde mit dir geh'n
berlin   raucheisen   lp: urania URLP 7013
4 may   lp: acanta 40.23503
1943   cd: melodram MEL 27050

cornelius **morgenlied (wenn die hähne frühe kräh'n)**
berlin　　　　　raucheisen　　　lp: urania URLP 7013
4 may　　　　　　　　　　　　　lp: classics club X 153
1943　　　　　　　　　　　　　　lp: acanta 40.23503
　　　　　　　　　　　　　　　　cd: melodram MEL 27050

verratene liebe, duet
berlin　　　　　raucheisen　　　lp: rococo 5363
16 november　　schmitt-walter　 lp: acanta 40.23503
1944

duets: am meer; der beste liebesbrief; in sternennacht; liebesprobe; scheiden und meiden; ein wort der liebe; zu den bergen hebt sich
berlin　　　　　raucheisen　　　lp: acanta 40.23503
16 november　　schmitt-walter
1944

CHRISTOPH WILLIBALD GLUCK (1714-1787)

orfeo ed euridice, excerpt (quest' asilo di placide palme)
leipzig	*role of euridice*	lp: eterna 820.898
29 november	leipzig radio	lp: acanta 22.221105
1954	orchestra	
	and chorus	
	masur	

orfeo ed euridice, excerpt (su e con me vieni!)
berlin	staatskapelle	78: electrola DB 6801
4 february	ludwig	lp: rococo 5203
1948	klose	lp: preiser LV 160
		lp: emi 1C147 28989-28990M
		lp: world records SHB 47
		cd: preiser 89167

orfeo ed euridice, excerpt (che fieri momento!)
berlin	statskapelle	78: electrola DB 6801
4 february	ludwig	lp: rococo 5203
1948	klose	lp: preiser LV 160
		lp: emi 1C147 28989-28990M
		lp: world records SHB 47
		cd: preiser 89167

EDUARD KUENNEKE (1885-1953)

die grosse sünderin, excerpt (immerzu singt dein herz meinem herzen zu)
berlin	staatskapelle	78: grammophon 15099
december	künneke	lp: historia H 696-697
1935	rosvaenge	lp: club 99-24
		lp: acanta 98.221776
		lp: preiser LV 516
		cd: preiser 89209

FRANZ LISZT (1811-1886)

wo weilt er?
berlin	raucheisen	lp: acanta 40.23563
3 february		cd: hamburger archiv für gesangskunst
1944		HAGLEM 1

GUSTAV MAHLER (1860-1911)

ich ging mit lust durch einen grünen wald/des knaben wunderhorn
berlin	ramin	lp: rococo 5320
7 april		*recorded at the singer's farewell recital*
1957		

WOLFGANG AMADEUS MOZART (1756-1791)

le nozze di figaro

berlin	*role of countess*	vhs video: defa musikfilm 10071
1949	staatskapelle	*soundtrack only for performance of the opera*
	and chorus	*in which other performers mime; however*
	rother	*ahlersmayer and domgraf-fassbänder do*
	berger	*appear in their roles*
	a.müller	
	klose	
	ahlersmayer	
	domgraf-fassbänder	

le nozze di figaro, excerpt (porgi amor)

berlin	staatskapelle	78: electrola DB 3462
24 february	seidler-winkler	45: electrola E 40074/7EW 118381
1938	*sung in the*	lp: emi 1C147 28989-28990M/EX 29 05983
	original italian	lp: preiser LV 101
		lp: world records SHB 47
		lp: arabesque 8028
		cd: emi CMS 763 7502
		cd: zyx music PD 50182
		cd: preiser 80902
berlin	berlin radio	lp: acanta 22.221105
1942	orchestra	cd: berlin classics BC 90142
	rother	
berlin	berlin radio	lp: rococo 5300
1 february	orchestra	
1945	heger	

mozart **le nozze di figaro, excerpt** (dove sono)

berlin	staatskapelle	78: electrola DB 3462
24 february	seidler-winkler	lp: victor LCT 6701
1938	*sung in the*	lp: hmv CSLP 503
	original italian	lp: emi 1C147 28989-28990M
		lp: rococo 5273
		lp: preiser LV 101
		lp: world records SHB 47
		lp: historia H 704-705
		lp: arabesque 8028
		cd: zyx music PD 50182
		cd: preiser 89025
berlin	städtische oper	unpublished reichsrundfunk broadcast
1942	orchestra	
	schmidt-isserstedt	
berlin	berlin radio	lp: rococo 5300
1 february	orchestra	lp: acanta 22.221105
1945	heger	cd: berlin classics BC 90142

mozart **die zauberflöte**

berlin	*role of pamina*	78: hmv DB 3465-3483/DB 8475-8493auto
8-15	berlin	78: electrola C 6371-6389
november	philharmonic	78: victor M 541-542
1937	favre chorus	45: victor WCT 56
	beecham	lp: victor LCT 6101
	berger	lp: hmv ALP 1273-1275
	rosvaenge	lp: electrola E 80471-80473/
	strienz	WCLP 616-618
	hüsch	lp: angel 6109
	grossmann	lp: world records SH 158-160
		lp: turnabout THS 65078-65080/ TV 4113-4115
		lp: calig CAL 30845-30846
		lp: emi 143 4653
		cd: emi CHS 761 0342
		cd: nimbus NI 7827-7828
		cd: pearl GEMMCDS 9371
		cd: melodram MEL 27056
		cd: dutton CDEA 5011
		cd: naxos 811.0127-0128
		cd: arkadia 78027
		excerpts
		lp: preiser LV 101
		lp: emi 1C147 28989-28990M
		lp: historia H 704-705
		lp: world records SHB 47
		cd: zyx music PD 50182
		cd: hamburger archiv für gesangskunst HAGLEM 2
		cd: preiser 89025
		recording completed in february and march 1938; issued in japan both by victor and toshiba
berlin	reichssender	unpublished reichsrundfunk broadcast
19 december	orchestra	
1937	and chorus	
	favre chorus	
	steiner	
	berger	
	w.ludwig	
	alsen	
	domgraf-fassbänder	
	hezel	

mozart **die zauberflöte, excerpt (bei männern welche liebe fühlen)**
berlin	berlin radio	lp: eterna 820 898
19 january	orchestra	lp: sonor 10-256333
1945	heger	lp: acanta BQ 21549/22.221105/
	schmitt-walter	22.214893
		cd: berlin classics BC 90142

some issues incorrectly dated 1942

das veilchen (ein veilchen auf der wiese stand)
berlin	raucheisen	lp: acanta 22.226379
22 september		lp: historia H 704-705
1942		cd: hamburger archiv für gesangskunst
		HAGLEM 1

CARL ORFF (1895-1982)

carmina burana, excerpt (in trutina)
berlin	staatskapelle	unpublished reichsrundfunk broadcast
26 january	and chorus	
1943	heger	

HANS PFITZNER (1869-1949)

studentenfahrt; trauerstille
berlin	raucheisen	unpublished reichsrundfunk broadcast
uncertain date		

RASCH

als ich dich kaum geseh'n; der mond ist aufgegangen
berlin	saal, harp	78: electrola DA 4486
1940	sänger, violin	lp: preiser LV 126
		lp: club 99-24
		cd: preiser 89115

FRANZ SCHUBERT (1797-1828)

am grabe anselmos (dass ich dich verloren habe)
berlin	raucheisen	78: grammophon 57085
1937		78: decca LY 6142
		lp: preiser LV 126
		lp: club 99-24
		cd: preiser 89115
		cd: dg 459 0082/459 0662

am see (sitz' ich im gras am glatten see)
berlin	raucheisen	unpublished reichsrundfunk broadcast
16 july		
1943		

ave maria/ellens gesang III
berlin	städtische oper	78: telefunken A 11153/A 099T
11 may	orchestra	45: telefunken UV 45515
1953	lutze	lp: telefunken BLE 14220
		lp: telefunken (canada) GF 63018

die blumensprache (es deuten die blumen)
berlin	raucheisen	lp: urania URLP 7013
10 june		lp: classics club X 153
1944		lp: rococo 5363
		cd: hamburger archiv für gesangskunst HAGLEM 1

der blumen schmerz (wie tönt es mir so schaurig)
berlin	raucheisen	lp: urania URLP 7013
10 june		lp: classics club X 153
1944		lp: rococo 5363
		cd: hamburger archiv für gesangskunst HAGLEM 1

cora an die sonne (nach so vielen trüben tagen)
berlin	raucheisen	lp: historia H 704-705
10 june		cd: hamburger archiv für gesangskunst
1944		HAGLEM 1

schubert **erster verlust (ach wer bringt die schönen tage?)**
berlin raucheisen lp: historia H 704-705
10 june lp: acanta 10.223051
1944 cd: hamburger archiv für gesangskunst
    HAGLEM 1

frühlingslied (die luft ist blau)
berlin raucheisen unpublished reichsrundfunk broadcast
22 september
1942

die gebüsche (es wehet kühl und leise)
berlin raucheisen lp: historia H 704-705
10 june cd: hamburger archiv für gesangskunst
1944   HAGLEM 1

heimliches lieben (o wenn deine lippen mich berühren)
berlin raucheisen lp: urania URLP 7047
16 july lp: rococo 5363
1943 lp: saga 7007
lp: acanta 10.223051/22.226379
cd: hamburger archiv für gesangskunst
    HAGLEM 1

schubert **das lied im grünen (ins grüne, ins grüne!)**
berlin   raucheisen   lp: historia H 704-705
10 june   lp: acanta 10.223051
1944   cd: hamburger archiv für gesangskunst
                                          HAGLEM 1

das mädchen (wie so innig, möcht' ich sagen)
berlin   raucheisen   unpublished reichsrundfunk broadcast
10 june
1944

nachtviolen, dunkle augen!
berlin   raucheisen   lp: rococo 5363
10 june
1944

seufzer (die nachtigall singt überall)
berlin   raucheisen   unpublished reichsrundfunk broadcast
22 september
1942

viola (schneeglöcklein, o schneeglöcklein!)
berlin   raucheisen   lp: urania URLP 7013
16 july   lp: classics club X 153
1943   cd: hamburger archiv für gesangskunst
                                          HAGLEM 1

wonne der wehmut (trocknet nicht, tränen der ewigen liebe!)
berlin   raucheisen   unpublished reichsrundfunk broadcast
10 june
1944

ROBERT SCHUMANN (1810-1856)

familiengemälde, duet
berlin   raucheisen   45: dg EPL 30 524
14 july   anders   lp: urania URLP 7047
1943   lp: saga 7007
                           lp: melodiya M10 41893-41894
                           cd: berlin classics BC 21672
                           cd: hamburger archiv für gesangskunst
                           HAGLEM 1

märzveilchen (der himmel wölbt sich rein und blau)
berlin   raucheisen   lp: record shop HSP 916
22 september   lp: saga 7007
1942   cd: hamburger archiv für gesangskunst
                           HAGLEM 1

schneeglöckchen (der schnee der gestern noch in flocken)
berlin   raucheisen   lp: urania URLP 7047
4 february   lp: record shop HSP 916
1944   lp: saga 7007
                           cd: hamburger archiv für gesangskunst
                           HAGLEM 1

schumann **die soldatenbraut (ach wenn's der könig auch wüsst'!)**
berlin raucheisen unpublished reichsrundfunk broadcast
4 february
1944

unterm fenster, duet
berlin raucheisen lp: urania URLP 7047
14 july anders lp: saga 7007
1943   lp: melodiya M10 41893-41894
   cd: hamburger archiv für gesangskunst
   HAGLEM 1

widmung (du meine seele, du mein herz!)
berlin raucheisen unpublished reichsrundfunk broadcast
10 june
1944

wiegenlied, duet
berlin raucheisen lp: urania URLP 7047
1944 anders lp: saga 7007
   lp: melodiya M10 41893-41894
   cd: hamburger archiv für gesangskunst
   HAGLEM 1

RICHARD STRAUSS (1864-1949)

arabella, excerpt (mein elemer!/ich möchte meinen fremden mann einmal noch sehen!)

berlin	*role of arabella*	78: electrola DB 5606
december	staatskapelle	lp: emi 1C147 28989-28990M/
1940	seidler-winkler	lp: world records SHB 47
		cd: emi CDH 566 7742
		cd: zyx music PD 50182
		cd: preiser 89950
		also issued on lp by preiser

arabella, excerpt (so wie sie sind!/und du wirst mein gebieter sein)

berlin	staatskapelle	78: electrola DB 5606
december	seidler-winkler	lp: electrola E 83393
1940	hüsch	lp: rococo 5203
		lp: preiser LV 160
		lp: emi 1C147 28989-28990M
		lp: world records SHB 47
		cd: emi CDH 566 7742
		cd: zyx music PD 50182
		cd: preiser 89167/89950

arabella, excerpt (das war sehr gut mandryka!)

berlin	städtische oper	lp: rococo 5300
5 july	orchestra	lp: eterna 820 898
1944	grüber	lp: historia H 704-705
	hüsch	lp: sonor 98.256901-256908
		lp: acanta 22.221105/98.221776
		cd: berlin classics BC 90142

strauss der rosenkavalier

dresden	*role of octavian*	lp: urania URLP 9201-9204
21-23	dresden	lp: acanta 40.23039
december	staatskapelle	*excerpts*
1950	and chorus	45: urania UREP 14
	bäumer	lp: urania ULP 90602/URLP 7062/8010
	richter	lp: saga XID 5177
	thomann	lp: historia H 704-705
	böhme	
	löbel	

der rosenkavalier, excerpt (da geht er hin, der schlechte aufgeblas'ne kerl!)

stuttgart	württemberg	78: dg LV 72 147-72 148
9-11	state orchestra	lp: dg LPM 18 011/89 698/479 012
october	leitner	lp: decca (usa) DL 9606
1951	milinkovic	

der rosenkavalier, excerpt (mir ist die ehre widerfahren)

berlin	berlin radio	lp: rococo 5300
20 january	orchestra	lp: historia H 677-678
1942	rother	cd: berlin classics BC 90142
	cebotari	

der rosenkavalier, excerpt (hab' mir's gelobt, ihn lieb zu haben)

berlin	staatskapelle	78: grammophon 67075
1936	krauss	78: decca CA 8238
	ursuleac	lp: preiser LV 1384
	berger	lp: diskophilia KG-U-1
		cd: dante LYS 019-021
		cd: preiser 89950
		cd: dg 459 0072/459 0662
berlin	berlin radio	lp: rococo 5300
20 january	orchestra	lp: acanta 22.21483-21484/KBF 21483/
1942	rother	22.221105
	buchner	cd: fonoteam CD 74506
	cebotari	cd: preiser 90222
stuttgart	württemberg	78: dg LV 72 121
9-11	state orchestra	45: dg EPL 30 141
october	leitner	lp: dg LPM 18 011/89 698/479 012
1951	trötschel	lp: decca (usa) DL 9606
	milinkovic	*lp editions begin at mein gott es war nicht mehr als eine farce!*

lemnitz sings role of marschallin in the 1951 stuttgart recording of rosenkavalier excerpts

strauss **der rosenkavalier, excerpt** (ist ein traum, kann nicht wirklich sein)
berlin	reichssender	lp: acanta 22.214903
june	orchestra	lp: bellaphon 23.119
1934	krauss	
	berger	

berlin	staatskapelle	78: grammophon 67075
1936	krauss	78: decca CA 8238
	berger	cd: nimbus NI 7848
		cd: dante LYS 019-021
		cd: dg 459 0072/459 0662
		cd: preiser 89035/89167/89950
		also issued on lp by preiser

berlin	berlin radio	lp: rococo 5300
20 january	orchestra	lp: acanta 22.221105/72.221792
1942	rother	lp: melodiya M10 47131 000
	cebotari	cd: preiser 90222

freundliche vision (nicht im schlafe hab' ich das geträumt)
berlin	ramin	lp: rococo 5320
7 april		*recorded at the singer's farewell recital*
1957		

PIOTR TCHAIKOVSKY (1840-1893)

the enchantress, excerpt (my fate is strange)
berlin	*role of natasha*	78: electrola DB 5624
1941	staatskapelle	lp: rococo 5203
	baltzer	lp: eterna (usa) 736
	rosvaenge	lp: preiser LV 43/LV 519
		lp: historia H 704-705
		lp: world records SHB 47
		cd: preiser 89211
		cd: hamburger archiv für gesangskunst HAGLEM 2
		cd: cantus classics CACD 500024

evgeny onegin, excerpt (tatiana's letter scene)
berlin	*role of tatiana*	lp: rococo 5363
1943	berlin radio	lp: eterna 820 898/822 604-822 605
	orchestra	lp: acanta 22.221105/98.221776
	rother	cd: berlin classics BC 90142
		cd: hamburger archiv für gesangskunst HAGLEM 2

berlin classics issue is dated 1946

GIUSEPPE VERDI (1813-1901)

aida, excerpt (ritorna vincitor!)

berlin	*role of aida*	78: grammophon 30018
25 january	staatskapelle	lp: rococo 5203
1937	f.a.schmidt	lp: preiser LV 101
		cd: preiser 89025

berlin	staatskapelle	78: electrola DB 6808
15-16	ludwig	lp: emi 1C147 28989-28990M
february	*sung in the*	lp: world records SHB 47
1948	*original italian*	cd: preiser 89167
		also issued on lp by preiser

aida, excerpt (o patria mia)

berlin	staatskapelle	78: grammophon 30018
25 january	f.a.schmidt	lp: rococo 5203
1937		lp: preiser LV 101
		cd: preiser 89025

berlin	staatskapelle	78: electrola DB 6808
20 february	ludwig	lp: emi 1C147 28989-28990M
1948	*sung in the*	lp: world records SHB 47
	original italian	cd: preiser 89167
		cd: dg 459 0052/459 0662
		also issued on lp by preiser

don carlo, excerpt (giustizia o sire!......to end of act four scene one)

berlin	*role of*	lp: rococo 5300
24 june	*elisabetta*	lp: acanta 10.223181/BB 22318/
1942	berlin radio	22.21483-21484/KBF 21488/
	orchestra	22.221105
	rother	cd: preiser 90257
	klose	cd: hamburger archiv für gesangskunst
	hann	HAGLEM 2
	ahlersmayer	

verdi otello, excerpt (gia nella notte densa)

berlin	*role of*	78: electrola DB 4668
april	*desdemona*	78: victor M 860
1939	staatskapelle	lp: preiser LV 102
	seidler-winkler	lp: emi 1C147 28989-28990M
	ralf	lp: historia H 704-705
		lp: world records SHB 47
		cd: emi CDH 566 7742
		cd: preiser 89077
		cd: zyx music PD 50182
		cd: hamburger archiv für gesangskunst HAGLEM 2

otello, excerpt (piangea cantando/ave maria)

berlin	staatskapelle	78: electrola DB 4595
november	seidler-winkler	78: victor M 860
1938		lp: rococo 5273
		lp: preiser LV 101
		lp: emi 1C147 28989-28990M
		lp: world records SHB 47
		cd: emi CDH 566 7742
		cd: preiser 89025
		cd: zyx music PD 50182
		ave maria only
		lp: emi EX 29 10753

otello, excerpt (poi mi giudavi?)

berlin	unknown	unpublished video recording
1943	orchestra and	*soundtrack recording only for the film*
	conductor	*altes herz wird wieder jung*
	lorenz	

il trovatore, excerpt (tacea la notte placida)

berlin	*role of leonora*	78: electrola DB 7656
1942	staatskapelle	lp: rococo 5203
	orthmann	lp: emi 1C147 28989-28990M
		cd: zyx music PD 50182
		cd: preiser 89167
		also issued on lp by preiser

il trovatore, excerpt (d'amor sull' ali rosee)
berlin	staatskapelle	78: electrola DB 7656
1942	orthmann	lp: rococo 5203
		lp: emi 1C147 28989-28990M
		cd: zyx music PD 50182
		cd: preiser 89167

also issued on lp by preiser

il trovatore, excerpt (mira d' acerbe lagrime)
berlin	berlin radio	lp: rococo 5300
19 january	orchestra	lp: somerset 689
1945	heger	lp: acanta 22.221105
	schmitt-walter	cd: berlin classics BC 90142
		cd: hamburger archiv für gesangskunst HAGLEM 2

BERNHARD VLIES (1770)

wiegenlied (schlafe mein prinzchen)
berlin	klust	78: electrola DA 5506
18 february		lp: world records SHB 47
1948		

RICHARD WAGNER (1813-1883)

lohengrin
leipzig	*role of elsa*	unpublished reichsrundfunk broadcast
16 january	reichssender	
1938	orchestra	
	and chorus	
	weisbach	
	rünger	
	seider	
	manowarda	
	schöffler	

lohengrin, excerpt (einsam in trüben tagen)
berlin	staatskapelle	78: grammophon 35081
1937	schüler	78: decca LY 6144
		lp: rococo 5203
		lp: preiser LV 101
		lp: historia H 704-705
		cd: voce della luna VL 20002
		cd: preiser 89025
		cd: hamburger archiv für gesangskunst HAGLEM 3
		also issued on lp by dg

wagner **lohengrin, excerpt (euch lüften die mein klagen)**

berlin	staatskapelle	78: grammophon 35081
1937	schüler	78: decca LY 6144
		lp: rococo 5273
		lp: preiser LV 101
		cd: voce della luna VL 20002
		cd: preiser 9025

berlin	staatskapelle	lp: world records SHB 47
30 january	ludwig	lp: emi 1C147 28989-28990M
1948	klose	cd: emi CDH 566 7742
		cd: voce della luna VL 20002
		cd: preiser 89167
		cd: hamburger archiv für gesangskunst HAGLEM 3

unpublished electrola 78rpm recording; extract continu as far as es gibt ein glück das ohne reu' elsa wer ruft? only
lp: preiser LV 160
lp: emi EX 29 02123
HAGLEM 3 incorrectly dated 1942 and incorrectly names conductor as schüler

wagner **lohengrin, excerpt (das süsse lied verhallt)**
berlin	staatskapelle	78: electrola DB 4667
april	seidler-winkler	lp: emi 1C147 28989-28990M/RLS 7711
1939	ralf	lp: world records SHB 47
		lp: preiser LV 102
		lp: historia H 704-705
		cd: pearl GEMMCD 9926
		cd: emi CDH 566 7742
		cd: voce della luna VL 20002
		cd: preiser 89022
		RLS 7711 incorrectly dated july 1939

berlin	berlin radio	lp: urania URLP 7019
15 december	orchestra	lp: eterna 820 898/821 873
1944	rother	lp: acanta 22.221105
	völker	lp: rca RL 30439
		cd: voce della luna VL 20002
		cd: berlin classics BC 90142
		cd: pilz CD 78007
		cd: radio years RY 76
		cd: hamburger archiv für gesangskunst HAGLEM 3

lohengrin, excerpt (in fernem land.....to end of opera)
berlin	berlin radio	lp: acanta 98.221776
15 december	orchestra	cd: hamburger archiv für gesangskunst
1944	and chorus	HAGLEM 3
	rother	*acanta issue commences only at mein lieber schwan*
	rünger	
	völker	
	hofmann	

wagner **die meistersinger von nürnberg**

dresden	*role of eva*	lp: urania URLP 206
24 april-	dresden	lp: vox OPBX 142
2 may	staatskapelle	cd: myto MCD 961.138
1951	and chorus	*excerpts*
	kempe	lp: classics club X 161
	walther-sacks	lp: vox OPL 350/PL 15100
	aldenhoff	lp: saga XID 5117/XID 5290/STXID 5290
	unger	lp: acanta 22.220281/22.292673/
	frantz	DE 29269/40.23502
	böhme	
	pflanzl	

die meistersinger von nürnberg, extended fragments including guten abend meister, o sachs mein freund and selig wie die sonne

nürnberg	vienna	lp: ed smith UORC 224
5 september	philharmonic	lp: private issue (japan) JP 1143-1144
1938	vienna opera	cd: palette (japan) PAL 2007-2008
	and nürnberg	cd: koch 3-1452-2
	choirs	*guten abend meister*
	furtwängler	lp: acanta 40.23502
	berglund	cd: acanta 44.1055
	laholm	cd: grammofono AB 78610
	zimmermann	cd: iron needle IN 1364-1365
	bockelmann	*guest performance by vienna staatsoper*
	fuchs	
	manowarda	

wagner die meistersinger von nürnberg, excerpt (morgenlich leuchtend/keiner wie du so hold zu werben weiss!)

london	london	78: columbia LX 646
20 may	philharmonic	78: columbia (usa) X 87
1936	covent garden	lp: hmv (sweden) SCLP 1022
	chorus	lp: ed smith EJS 444
	beecham	lp: rococo 5233
	ralf	lp: emi RLS 742/RLS 7711/EX 29 02123
	bockelmann	cd: dutton CDLX 7007
		cd: hamburger archiv für gesangskunst HAGLEM 3

tannhäuser, excerpt (dich teure halle!)

berlin	*role of*	78: grammophon 15079/67058
1934	*elisabeth*	78: decca CA 8243
	staatskapelle	lp: rococo 5273
	blech	lp: preiser LV 101
		cd: voce della luna VL 20002
		cd: nimbus NI 7848
		cd: preiser 89025

berlin	berlin radio	lp: urania URLP 7019
5 february	orchestra	lp: acanta 22.221105
1942	rother	cd: voce della luna VL 20002
		cd: hamburger archiv für gesangskunst HAGLEM 3

tannhäuser, excerpt (allmächt'ge jungfrau)

berlin	staatskapelle	78: grammophon 15079/67058
1934	blech	78: decca CA 8243
		lp: rococo 5203
		lp: preiser LV 101
		lp: historia H 704-705
		cd: voce della luna VL 20002
		cd: preiser 89025

berlin	staatskapelle	78: electrola DB 6809
2 february	ludwig	lp: emi 1C147 28989-28990M
1948		lp: world records SHB 47
		cd: emi CDH 566 7742
		cd: voce della luna VL 20002
		cd: preiser 89167
		cd: hamburger archiv für gesangskunst HAGLEM 3

wagner **die walküre, excerpt (act one scene one and beginning of scene two)**

buenos aires 1950	teatro colon orchestra böhm suthaus greindl	unpublished radio broadcast

der engel/wesendonk-lieder

berlin 1937	raucheisen	78: grammophon 57084 78: decca LY 6141 lp: preiser LV 126 lp: club 99-24 cd: voce della luna VL 20002 cd: preiser 89115
berlin 1943	raucheisen	lp: urania URLP 7019 cd: voce della luna VL 20002
berlin 7 july 1944	staatskapelle heger	cd: acanta CD 43275 cd: voce della luna VL 20002
berlin 20 january 1955	berlin radio orchestra abendroth	cd: arlecchino ARL 93 *orchestra incorrectly described as leipzig radio orchestra and incorrectly dated 1950*
berlin 7 april 1957	ramin	lp: rococo 5300 *recorded at the singer's farewell recital*

wagner stehe still!/wesendonk-lieder

berlin 1937	raucheisen	78: grammophon 57084 78: decca LY 6141 lp: preiser LV 126 lp: club 99-24 cd: voce della luna VL 20002 cd: preiser 89115
berlin 1943	raucheisen	lp: urania URLP 7019 cd: voce della luna VL 20002
berlin 7 july 1944	staatskapelle heger	cd: acanta CD 43275 cd: voce della luna VL 20002
berlin 20 january 1955	berlin radio orchestra abendroth	cd: arlecchino ARL 93 *orchestra incorrectly described as leipzig radio orchestra and incorrectly dated 1950*

im treibhaus/wesendonk-lieder

berlin 1936	raucheisen	78: grammophon 57028 78: decca CA 8253 lp: preiser LV 126 lp: club 99-24 cd: voce della luna VL 20002 cd: preiser 89115
berlin 1943	raucheisen	lp: urania URLP 7019 cd: voce della luna VL 20002
berlin 7 july 1944	staatskapelle heger	cd: acanta CD 43275 cd: voce della luna VL 20002
berlin 20 january 1955	berlin radio orchestra abendroth	cd: arlecchino ARL 93 *orchestra incorrectly described as leipzig radio orchestra and incorrectly dated 1950*
berlin 7 april 1957	ramin	lp: rococo 5300 *recorded at the singer's farewell recital*

wagner **schmerzen/wesendonk-lieder**

berlin 1937	raucheisen	78: grammophon 57085 78: decca LY 6142 lp: preiser LV 126 lp: club 99-24 cd: voce della luna VL 20002 cd: preiser 89115
berlin 1943	raucheisen	lp: urania URLP 7019 cd: voce della luna VL 20002
berlin 7 july 1944	staatskapelle heger	lp: historia H 704-705 cd: voce della luna VL 20002 cd: acanta CD 43275 *historia incorrectly dated 1946*
berlin 20 january 1955	berlin radio orchestra abendroth	cd: arlecchino ARL 93 *orchestra incorrectly described as leipzig radio* *orchestra and incorrectly dated 1950*
berlin 7 april 1957	ramin	lp: rococo 5300 *recorded at the singer's farewell recital*

wagner **träume/wesendonk-lieder**

berlin 1936	raucheisen	78: grammophon 57028 78: decca CA 8253 lp: preiser LV 126 lp: club 99-24 cd: voce della luna VL 20002 cd: preiser 89115 cd: dg 459 0082/459 0662 *dg edition dated 1937*
berlin 1943	raucheisen	lp: urania URLP 7019 cd: voce della luna VL 20002
berlin 7 july 1944	staatskapelle heger	lp: historia H 704-705 cd: voce della luna VL 20002 cd: acanta CD 43275 *historia incorrectly dated 1946*
berlin 20 january 1955	berlin radio orchestra abendroth	cd: arlecchino ARL 93 *orchestra incorrectly described as leipzig radio* *orchestra and incorrectly dated 1950*
berlin 7 april 1957	ramin	lp: rococo 5300 *recorded at the singer's farewell recital*

CARL MARIA VON WEBER (1786-1826)

der freischütz

berlin 20 december 1936	*role of agathe* reichssender orchestra and chorus steiner beilke wittrisch bohnen witting böhme	lp: ed smith UORC 352 *excerpts* cd: gebhardt JGCD 00151

weber **der freischütz, excerpt (wie nahte mir der schlummer/leise leise)**

berlin	staatskapelle	78: grammophon 15081
1934	blech	78: decca CA 8233/LY 6108
		lp: rococo 5273
		lp: club 99-24
		lp: preiser LV 101
		lp: acanta 98.221776
		leise leise only
berlin	staatskapelle	78: electrola DB 5549
1939	seidler-winkler	45: electrola E 40074/7EW 118381
		lp: preiser LV 160
		lp: emi 1C147 28989-28990M
		lp: world records SHB 47
		cd: emi CDH 566 7742
		cd: zyx music PD 50182
		cd: preiser 89025
salzburg	vienna	cd: radio years RY 70
3 august	philharmonic	cd: koch 3-1467-2
1939	knappertsbusch	
berlin	berlin radio	lp: acanta 22.221105
1942	orchestra	cd: hamburger archiv für gesangskunst
	rother	HAGLEM 2
berlin	staatskapelle	78: electrola DB 6802/DB 11523
20 february	ludwig	*the two issues contain different takes of side one*
1948		

weber **der freischütz, excerpt (und ob die wolke)**

berlin	staatskapelle	78: grammophon 15081
1934	blech	78: decca CA 8233/LY 6108
		lp: rococo 5203
		lp: preiser LV 101
		cd: preiser 89025/89403
salzburg	vienna	cd: radio years RY 70
3 august	philharmonic	cd: koch 3-1467-2
1939	knappertsbusch	
berlin	berlin radio	lp: eterna 820 898
1944	orchestra	lp: historia H 704-705
	rother	cd: berlin classics BC 90142
		cd: hamburger archiv für gesangskunst HAGLEM 2
		berlin classics incorrectly dated 1953
berlin	staatskapelle	78: electrola DA 1881/DA 5509
15-16	ludwig	lp: emi 1C147 28989-28990M
february		lp: world records SHB 47
1948		cd: emi CDH 566 7742
		cd: preiser 89167

HUGO WOLF (1860-1903)

agnes/mörike-lieder
berlin   raucheisen   lp: acanta 23.580
16 november   cd: hamburger archiv für gesangskunst
1944   HAGLEM 1

auf eine christblume/mörike-lieder
berlin   raucheisen   lp: electrola E 73398
14 october   cd: emi CHS 566 6402
1937   *unpublished electrola 78rpm recording*

date   raucheisen   unpublished reichsrundfunk broadcast
uncertain

die bekehrte/goethe-lieder
berlin   seidler-winkler   78: electrola DA 4469
1939   lp: rococo 5273
                                           lp: club 99-24
                                           lp: preiser LV 126
                                           cd: preiser 89115

frohe botschaft (hielt die allerschönste herrin)
date   raucheisen   unpublished reichsrundfunk broadcast
uncertain

gebet/mörike-lieder
berlin   ramin   lp: rococo 5300
7 april   *recorded at the singer's farewell recital*
1957

in der frühe/mörike-lieder
berlin　　　　　raucheisen　　　lp: electrola E 73398
14 october　　　　　　　　　　lp: world records SHB 47
1937　　　　　　　　　　　　　lp: emi RLS 759/1C163 03991-03997M
　　　　　　　　　　　　　　　cd: emi CHS 566 6402
　　　　　　　　　　　　　　　cd: preiser 89115
　　　　　　　　　　　　　　　unpublished electrola 78rpm recording

berlin　　　　　ramin　　　　　lp: rococo 5300
7 april　　　　　　　　　　　　*recorded at the singer's farewell recital*
1957

die kleine/eichendorff-lieder
berlin　　　　　raucheisen　　　78: electrola DA 4491
1940　　　　　　　　　　　　　lp: rococo 5273
　　　　　　　　　　　　　　　lp: club 99-24
　　　　　　　　　　　　　　　lp: historia H 704-705
　　　　　　　　　　　　　　　lp: preiser LV 126
　　　　　　　　　　　　　　　cd: preiser 89115

der knabe und das immlein/mörike-lieder
berlin　　　　　raucheisen　　　lp: urania URLP 7013
16 march　　　　　　　　　　　lp: classics club X 153
1943　　　　　　　　　　　　　lp: rococo 5363
　　　　　　　　　　　　　　　lp: acanta 23.580
　　　　　　　　　　　　　　　cd: hamburger archiv für gesangskunst
　　　　　　　　　　　　　　　　　HAGLEM 1

liebesfrühling (wie oft schon ward es frühling)
date　　　　　　raucheisen　　　unpublished reichsrundfunk broadcast
uncertain

lied des transferierten zettels (die schwalbe die den sommer bringt)
date　　　　　　raucheisen　　　unpublished reichsrundfunk broadcast
uncertain

nachtgruss (in dem himmel ruht die erde)
berlin　　　　　raucheisen　　　78: electrola DA 4491
1940　　　　　　　　　　　　　lp: rococo 5273
　　　　　　　　　　　　　　　lp: preiser LV 126
　　　　　　　　　　　　　　　cd: preiser 89115

date　　　　　　raucheisen　　　unpublished reichsrundfunk broadcast
uncertain

wolf **neue liebe/mörike-lieder**
date   raucheisen   unpublished reichsrundfunk broadcast
uncertain

peregrina I and II/mörike-lieder
date   raucheisen   unpublished reichsrundfunk broadcast
uncertain

sankt nepomuks vorabend/goethe-lieder
berlin   raucheisen   lp: electrola E 73398
14 october   lp: world records SHB 47
1937   lp: emi RLS 759/1C163 03991-03997M
                                                   cd: emi CHS 566 6402
                                                   cd: preiser 89115
                                                 unpublished electrola 78rpm recording

schlafendes jesuskind/mörike-lieder
berlin   raucheisen   lp: electrola E 73398
14 october   lp: world records SHB 47
1937   cd: emi CHS 566 6402
                                               cd: record collector TRC 8
                                             cd: preiser 89115
                                             unpublished electrola 78rpm recording

schlummerlied (sususu du bienchen!)
berlin   raucheisen   lp: urania URLP 7013
1943   lp: classics club X 122
                                             lp: rococo 5363
                                             cd: hamburger archiv für gesangskunst
                                                    HAGLEM 1
                                             incorrectly described by urania as wiegenlied

der schwalbe heimkehr (wenn die schwalben heimwärts ziehen)
date   raucheisen   unpublished reichsrundfunk broadcast
uncertain

wolf skolie (reich' den pokal mir!)
date　　　　　　raucheisen　　　　unpublished reichsrundfunk broadcast
uncertain

die spröde/goethe-lieder
berlin　　　　　seidler-winkler　　78: electrola DA 4469
1939　　　　　　　　　　　　　　lp: rococo 5273
　　　　　　　　　　　　　　　　lp: club 99-24
　　　　　　　　　　　　　　　　lp: historia H 704-705
　　　　　　　　　　　　　　　　lp: preiser LV 126
　　　　　　　　　　　　　　　　cd: preiser 89115

verborgenheit/mörike-lieder
berlin　　　　　ramin　　　　　　lp: rococo 5300
7 april　　　　　　　　　　　　　*recorded at the singer's farewell recital*
1957

weint nicht ihr äuglein/spanisches liederbuch
date　　　　　　raucheisen　　　　unpublished reichsrundfunk broadcast
uncertain

wer tat deinem füsslein weh?/spanisches liederbuch
date　　　　　　raucheisen　　　　unpublished reichsrundfunk broadcast
uncertain

wiegenlied im sommer (vom berg hinabgestiegen)
berlin　　　　　raucheisen　　　　78: electrola DB 3326
14 october　　　　　　　　　　　lp: rococo 5273
1937　　　　　　　　　　　　　　lp: preiser LV 126
　　　　　　　　　　　　　　　　lp: world records SHB 47
　　　　　　　　　　　　　　　　lp: emi RLS 759/1C163 03991-03997M
　　　　　　　　　　　　　　　　cd: emi CHS 566 6402
　　　　　　　　　　　　　　　　cd: preiser 89115

berlin　　　　　klust　　　　　　electrola unpublished
18 february
1948

wolf **wiegenlied im winter (schlaf' ein mein süsses kind!)**
berlin	raucheisen	lp: electrola E 73398
14 october		lp: world records SHB 47
1937		lp: emi RLS 759/1C163 03991-03997M
		cd: emi CHS 566 6402
		cd: preiser 89115
		unpublished electrola 78rpm recording

wohin mit der freud'? (ach du klarblauer himmel!)
date uncertain	raucheisen	unpublished reichsrundfunk broadcast

zitronenfalter im april/mörike-lieder
berlin	raucheisen	lp: urania URLP 7013
16 march		lp: classics club X 153
1943		lp: rococo 5363
		lp: acanta 23.580
		cd: hamburger archiv für gesangskunst HAGLEM 1

franz völker
1899-1965

FRANZ ABT (1819-1885)

gute nacht du mein herziges kind (all' abend bevor ich zur ruhe geh')
berlin	unknown	78: grammophon 21935
1928	orchestra and conductor	lp: dg 88 015
		dg incorrectly describes this item as an aria from lehar's friederike

im herzen hab' ich dich getragen
berlin	unknown	78: grammophon 21248
1928	orchestra and conductor	

o jugend wie bist du so schön! (die sonne leuchtet, der frühling blüht)
berlin	orchestra	78: grammophon 19909
1928	gurlitt	

o schwarzwald, o heimat!
berlin	orchestra	78: grammophon 22737
1929	snaga	cd: franz-völker-kreis CDFVK 1

EUGEN D'ALBERT (1864-1932)

tiefland, excerpts (ich grüss' noch einmal meine berge; mein leben wagt' ich drum)
berlin	*role of pedro*	78: grammophon 67685
1940	staatskapelle	lp: dg 88 015
	steeger	lp: scala (usa) 863
		cd: preiser 89070
		also issued on lp by preiser

ERNEST ARNOLD (1900)

da draussen in der wachau
berlin	orchestra	78: grammophon 47064
1 october	schütze	lp: rococo 5293
1936		cd: franz-völker-kreis CDFVK 1

VLADIMIR BAKALAINIKOW (1900)

habe mitleid mit mir! (wo ich immer auch bin)
berlin   unknown   78: grammophon 21933
1928   orchestra and
                   conductor

ERNEST BALL (1878-1927)

lieb' mich und die welt ist mein! (ich wandle wie im traum einher)
berlin   orchestra   78: grammophon 24617
1931   melichar

wo zwei augen dich selig begrüssen (ich zog in der welt umher)
berlin   unknown   78: grammophon 7001
1928   orchestra and
                   conductor

GIUSEPPE BECCE (1900)

du bist mein glück, from film of the same name
berlin   orchestra   78: grammophon 47065
1936   schütze   cd: franz-völker-kreis RR 501

LUDWIG VAN BEETHOVEN (1770-1827)

fidelio, excerpt (gott welch' dunkel hier!/in des lebens frühlingstagen)
berlin	*role of florestan*	78: grammophon 15452/27311/95984
1933	staatskapelle	lp: preiser LV 78
	melichar	lp: dg 2700 708
		lp: top classic TC 9065
		lp: historia H 644-645
		lp: scala (usa) 863
		cd: preiser 89070/89401
		cd: zyx music PC 50022

RALPH BENATZKY (1884-1957)

die drei muskatiere, excerpt (wenn du treulos bist)
berlin	unknown	78: grammophon 22709
1929	orchestra and conductor	

IRVING BERLIN (1888-1989)

always
berlin	unknown	78: grammophon 19788
1928	orchestra and conductor	

GEORGES BIZET (1838-1875)

carmen, excerpt (la fleur que tu m' avais jetée)
berlin	*role of josé*	78: grammophon 67015/95037/95436
1928	unknown	45: dg EPL 30 176
	orchestra and	lp: preiser LV 78
	conductor	lp: dg 88 015
		lp: top classic BB 45005

CARL BOHM (1844-1920)

trinkspruch (die berge glüh'n im sonnenschein)
berlin   orchestra   78: grammophon 21935
1928   gurlitt

JOHANNES BRAHMS (1833-1897)

wiegenlied (guten abend gut' nacht)
berlin   raucheisen   78: grammophon 23084
1929   cd: preiser 89997

EDUARDO DI CAPUA (1865-1917)

o sole mio
berlin   unknown   78: grammophon 27151
1929   orchestra and
                 conductor

CARL CLEWING (1884-1954)

alle tage ist kein sonntag
berlin   orchestra   78: grammophon 10780/23637
1930   melichar

GEORGE CLUTSAM (1866-1951)

my curly headed baby
berlin orchestra 78: grammophon 19787
1928 gurlitt

TEODORO COTTRAU (1827-1879)

santa lucia (süsses neapel, holdsel'ge wonne!)
berlin orchestra 78: grammophon 10449/24419/24790
1931 melichar

WILLY CZERNIK (1901)

am koblenzer eck (zu koblenz am eck)
berlin	orchestra	78: grammophon 19910
1928	gurlitt	cd: franz-völker-kreis CDFVK 1

aufzug
frankfurt	czernik, piano	unpublished radio broadcast
14 august		
1951		

es reiten die kosaken aus nowgorod (sie nennen wohl nowgorod)
berlin	staatskapelle	78: grammophon 27062
1928	snaga	

leicht gepäck (ich bin ein freier mann und singe)
berlin	staatskapelle	78: grammophon 27062
1928	snaga	

liebesbrief am grammophon (uns trennen tausende von meilen)
berlin	staatskapelle	78: grammophon 27206
1929	weigert	

mon reve familier
frankfurt	czernik, piano	unpublished radio broadcast
14 august		
1951		

die nachtigall (das macht, es hat die nachtigall)
berlin   orchestra   78: grammophon 21997
1928   gurlitt

o holde nacht (fühl' ich den abend bald nahen)
berlin   orchestra   78: grammophon 21997
1928   gurlitt

und es wird kommen ein sommertag
frankfurt   czernik, piano   unpublished radio broadcast
14 august
1951

was blumen sprechen (lockende sommernacht!)
berlin   orchestra   78: grammophon 19910
1928   gurlitt

ANTONIN DVORAK (1841-1904)

love songs op 38
frankfurt   czernik   unpublished radio broadcast
14 august
1951

RALPH ERWIN

schenk' mir doch nie eine frau (was kost' die welt)
berlin staatskapelle 78: grammophon 27206
1930 weigert cd: franz-völker-kreis RR 501

leb wohl schwarzbraunes mägdelein
berlin orchestra 78: grammophon 23637
1930 melichar

ich küsse ihre hand madame (madame ich lieb' sie)
berlin unknown 78: grammophon 21810
1928 orchestra and cd: franz-völker-kreis RR 501
 conductor

EDMUND EYSLER (1874-1949)

bruder straubinger, excerpt (küssen ist keine sünd')
berlin unknown 78: grammophon 19786
1928 orchestra and cd: preiser 89221
 conductor

der lachende ehemann, excerpt (fein schmeckt der wein)
berlin unknown 78: grammophon 19786
1928 orchestra and cd: preiser 89221
 conductor

PHILIPP ZU EULENBURG (1847-1921)

monatsrose/rosenlieder
berlin   raucheisen   78: grammophon 22736
1929

rankende rose/rosenlieder
berlin   vultee   78: grammophon 23957
1931

seerose/rosenlieder
berlin   vultee   78: grammophon 23958
1931

weisse und rote rose/rosenlieder
berlin   vultee   78: grammophon 23957
1931

wilde rose/rosenlieder
berlin   raucheisen   78: grammophon 22736
1929

HUGO FELIX (1866-1934)

die kätzchen, excerpt (unter dem lindenbaum)
berlin   unknown   78: grammophon 19996
1928   orchestra and
                     conductor

ERNST FISCHER (1900-1975)

sonntag am rhein (es läuten die glocken am rhein)
berlin   unknown   78: grammophon 19996
1928   orchestra and
                conductor

vergangene zeit (es lag eine heimliche schänke vor jahren am rhein)
berlin   unknown   78: grammophon 21934
1928   orchestra and
                conductor

RUDOLF FRIML (1879-1972)

rose marie, excerpt (über die prärie)
berlin   staatskapelle   78: grammophon 10270
20 october   melichar   cd: preiser 89221
1934

JAN KAROL GALL (1856-1912)

mädchen mit dem roten mündchen
berlin   unknown   78: grammophon 22739
1929   orchestra and
                conductor

STANISLAO GASTALDON (1861-1939)

musica proibita (vom balkon jeden abend)
berlin	unknown	78: grammophon 19787
1928	orchestra and	cd: franz-völker-kreis RR 501
	conductor	

berlin	unknown	78: grammophon 47065
7 october	orchestra and	
1936	conductor	

HENRY ERNEST GEEHL (1881-1961)

for you alone
berlin	unknown	78: grammophon 21933
1928	orchestra and	
	conductor	

WALTER WILHELM GOETZE (1883-1961)

o schöne zeit (es war ein sonntag hell und klar)
berlin	orchestra	78: grammophon 21996
1928	gurlitt	

CHARLES GOUNOD (1818-1893)

chanson de printemps
berlin	staatskapelle	78: grammophon 24200
1931	zweig	

PAUL GRAENER (1872-1944)

hochzeitsspruch for soprano, tenor and orchestra
berlin	staatskapelle	unpublished reichsrundfunk broadcast
10 april	gräner	*performance at wedding ceremony of hermann göring*
1935	ursuleac	*and emmy sondermann*

ALEXANDER GRETCHANINOV (1864-1956)

homeland
berlin unknown 78: grammophon 19793
1928 orchestra and
  conductor

EDVARD GRIEG (1843-1907)

i love thee
berlin orchestra 78: grammophon 21041
1927 heidenreich

berlin städtische oper unpublished reichsrundfunk broadcast
7 october orchestra
1944 steinkopf

WILHELM GROSZ (1894-1939)

wein-walzer (wer ein wenig mich kennt, weiss ich bin abstinent!)
berlin paul godwin- 78: grammophon 10603/25200
1930 künstler-
  orchester

FRANZ GROTHE (1908-1982)

alles für euch schöne frauen, from the film tingel-tangel
berlin unknown 78: grammophon 23838
1931 orchestra and cd: franz-völker-kreis RR 501
  conductor

JACQUES HALEVY (1799-1862)

la juive, excerpt (dieu de nos peres!)
berlin	*role of eleazar*	78: grammophon 27328
1933	staatskapelle	lp: preiser LV 78
	melichar	cd: preiser 89070

la juive, excerpt (quand du seigneur)
berlin	staatskapelle	78: grammophon 27328
1933	melichar	lp: preiser LV 78/LV 500
		cd: preiser 89005/89401

ROBERT HEGER (1886-1978)

die weisse rose
berlin	raucheisen	unpublished reichsrundfunk broadcast
13 november		
1944		

CARL HEINS

zwei dunkle augen, ein purpurner mund
berlin	unknown	78: grammophon 22739
1929	orchestra and	
	conductor	

WERNER RICHARD HEYMANN (1896-1961)

der kongress tanzt, excerpt (das gibt's nur einmal)
berlin	ilja-livschakoff-	78: grammophon 24344
1931	tanzorchester	cd: franz-völker-kreis RR 501

der kongress tanzt, excerpt (das muss ein stück vom himmel sein)
berlin	ilja-livschakoff	78: grammophon 24344
1931	tanzorchester	lp: rococo 5293
		cd: franz-völker-kreis RR 501

EUGEN HILDACH (1849-1924)

der lenz (die finken schlagen, der lenz ist da!)
berlin   orchestra   78: grammophon 21040
1927   heidenreich

in meiner heimat wird es jetzt frühling
berlin   heidenreich,   78: grammophon 21041
1927   piano

FREDERICK HOLLAENDER (1896-1976)

die zwölf frauen des jephat, excerpt (kirschen in nachbars garten)
berlin   unknown   78: grammophon 22738
1929   orchestra and   cd: preiser 89221
                conductor

der vorschuss auf die seligkeit (wenn man verliebt ist)
berlin   orchestra   78: grammophon 24740
1931   melichar

OTTO HOESER (1897-1959)

deutschland erwache, es ist frühling! (trotzige burgen, verfallene mauern!)
berlin   paul-godwin-   78: grammophon 23316
1930   künstler-   cd: franz-völker-kreis CDFVK 1
                orchester

deutschland du darfst nicht untergeh'n! (deutschland du land so herrlich schön!)
berlin   staatskapelle   78: grammophon 24806
1932   melichar

ENGELBERT HUMPERDINCK (1854-1921)

am rhein (wenn im sonnigen herbst die traube schwillt)
berlin orchestra 78: grammophon 19729
1927 heidenreich

ADOLF JENSEN (1837-1879)

murmelndes lüftchen
berlin vultee 78: grammophon 23958
1931

o lass' dich halten, gold'ne stunde!
berlin unknown 78: grammophon 24241
1931 orchestra and
conductor

AL JOLSON (1886-1950)

sonny boy
berlin unknown 78: grammophon 22644
1929 orchestra and
conductor

WALTER JURMANN (born 1903)

ninon, from the film ein lied für dich
berlin orchestra 78: grammophon 25115
1933 schütze cd: tmk (germany) TMK 7785

signora komm' zu mir! from the film ein lied für dich
berlin orchestra 78: grammophon 25115
1933 schütze

EMMERICH KALMAN (1882-1953)

die zirkusprinzessin, excerpt (zwei märchenaugen)
berlin orchestra 78: grammophon 19970
1928 prüwer cd: preiser 89221

BRONISLAW KAPER (1902-1983)

tränen weint jede frau so gern (frauen versteh'n mit ihren reizen zu spielen)
berlin   gurlitt   78: grammophon 22240
1929

WILHELM KIENZL (1857-1941)

der evangelimann, excerpt (selig sind die verfolgung leiden)
berlin   *role of mathias*   78: grammophon 95037
1928   unknown   lp: preiser LV 206
         orchestra and   lp: dg 88 015
         conductor   lp: top classic BB 45005
                  lp: gutenberg ASL 1331

EDUARD KUENNEKE (1885-1953)

es gibt nur eine liebe
berlin   orchestra   78: grammophon 25324/47113
1932   schütze

EDWARD LASSEN (1830-1904)

allerseelen (stell' auf den tisch die duftenden reseden)
berlin   orchestra   78: grammophon 22196
1928   gurlitt

ich hatte einst ein schönes vaterland
berlin   orchestra   78: grammophon 22196
1929   snaga   lp: rococo 5293

FRANZ LEHAR (1870-1948)

friederike, excerpt (o mädchen mein mädchen!)
berlin   unknown   *first version*
1928   orchestra and   78: grammophon 21811
        conductor   45: dg EPH 21 117
                                    lp: dg 88 015
                                    second version
                                    78: grammophon 19969
                                    78: decca LY 6024
                                    lp: rococo 5293
                                    cd: preiser 89221

friederike, excerpt (sah ein knab' ein röslein steh'n)
berlin   unknown   *first version*
1928   orchestra and   78: grammophon 21811
        conductor   lp: dg 88 015
                                    second version
                                    78: grammophon 19969
                                    78: decca LY 6024
                                    lp: rococo 5293
                                    cd: preiser 89221

giuditta, excerpt (schaut der mond abends spät)
berlin   staatskapelle   78: grammophon 25369/90207
1934   unknown   lp: eterna (usa) 723
        conductor   cd: preiser 89221
        kern

giuditta, excerpt (schön wie die blaue sommernacht)
berlin   staatskapelle   78: grammophon 25369/90207/90231
1934   unknown   lp: eterna (usa) 735
        conductor   cd: preiser 89221
        kern

giuditta, excerpt (du bist meine sonne)
berlin   staatskapelle   78: grammophon 25368/48033/
1934   unknown   90208/90231
        conductor   78: supraphon C 19124
                                    lp: rococo 5293
                                    cd: preiser 89221

lehar **giuditta, excerpt (freunde das leben ist lebenswert!)**
berlin	staatskapelle	78: grammophon 25368/48033/90208
1934	unknown	78: supraphon C 19124
	conductor	lp: rococo 5293
		cd: preiser 89221

der göttergatte (was ich längst erträumte)
berlin	orchestra	78: grammophon 10798/24740
1931	melichar	cd: preiser 89221

das land des lächelns, excerpt (dein ist mein ganzes herz)
berlin	orchestra	78: grammophon 22760
1929	snaga	cd: preiser 89221

berlin	staatskapelle	78: grammophon 48498/62803
11 june	unknown	lp: rococo 5293
1938	conductor	lp: dg 88 015
		cd: dg 459 0072/459 0662
		cd: preiser 89221
		also issued on lp by preiser

das land des lächelns, excerpt (immer nur lächeln)
berlin	orchestra	78: grammophon 22760
1929	snaga	78: decca PO 5015
		cd: preiser 89221

berlin	staatskapelle	78: grammophon 48498/62803
11 june	unknown	lp: rococo 5293
1938	conductor	lp: dg 88 015
		cd: preiser 89221
		cd: franz-völker-kreis RR 501
		also issued on lp by preiser

lehar **das land des lächelns, duets (bei einem tee en deux; wer hat die liebe uns ins herz gesenkt?)**
berlin orchestra 78: grammophon 22843
1929 snaga cd: preiser 89221
 kochhahn

die lustige witwe, excerpt (da geh' ich zu maxim!)
berlin orchestra grammophon unpublished
1928 gurlitt *test pressing in german rundfunkarchiv*

paganini, excerpt (gern hab' ich die frau'n geküsst)
berlin orchestra 78: grammophon 19682
1927 heidenreich cd: preiser 89221

der rastelbinder, excerpt (wenn zwei sich lieben)
berlin staatskapelle 78: grammophon 24177
1931 zweig lp: rococo 5293
 cd: preiser 89221

der zarewitsch, excerpt (wolgalied)
berlin orchestra 78: grammophon 15182/19970/
1928 prüwer 57414/566 304
 45: dg EPH 21 117
 lp: dg 88 015/635 067/49 109
 lp: rococo 5293
 cd: preiser 89221

der zarewitsch, excerpt (mädel wonniges mädel!)
berlin orchestra 78: grammophon 19730
1927 heidenreich cd: preiser 89221

RUGGIERO LEONCAVALLO (1858-1919)

i pagliacci, excerpt (un tal gioco)
berlin	*role of canio*	78: grammophon 90166
1930	staatskapelle	lp: preiser LV 206
	weigert	lp: gutenberg ASL 1331

i pagliacci, excerpt (vesti la giubba)
berlin	staatskapelle	78: grammophon 90166
1930	weigert	lp: preiser LV 206
		lp: top classic BB 45005
		lp: gutenberg ASL 1331
		cd: preiser 89005
vienna	vienna	lp: teletheater 120.841
19 january	philharmonic	
1934	alwin	

i pagliacci, excerpt (no pagliacco non son!)
vienna	vienna	cd: koch 3-1466-2
19 january	philharmonic	*this version continues as far as ah tu mi sfidi!*
1934	vienna opera	
	chorus	
	achsel	
	schipper	
	hammes	
berlin	staatskapelle	78: grammophon 67159/95494
25 october	schüler	45: dg EPL 30 169
1937		lp: preiser LV 1329
		cd: preiser 89070

mattinata
berlin	unknown	78: grammophon 15186/19793
1928	orchestra and	cd: dg 459 0052/459 0662
	conductor	

PAUL LINCKE (1866-1946)

frau luna, potpourri
berlin	volkstheater	78: grammophon 10370
1935	orchestra	
	and chorus	
	lincke	

heimlich still und leise
berlin	orchestra	78: grammophon 25064/47114
1931	melichar	

im reich der indra, excerpt (es war einmal)
berlin	orchestra	78: grammophon 19909
1928	gurlitt	cd: preiser 89221

nakiris hochzeit, excerpt (ob du mich liebst?)
berlin	orchestra	78: grammophon 10443/21651
1928	gurlitt	cd: preiser 89221

CARL LOEWE (1796-1869)

tom der reimer (der reimer thomas lag am bach)
berlin	altmann	78: grammophon 15462/57061/67350
1936		cd: preiser 89997

die uhr (ich trage stets eine uhr bei mir)
berlin	altmann	78: grammophon 15462/57061/67350
1936		cd: preiser 89230/89997

ALBERT LORTZING (1801-1851)

undine, excerpt (vater mutter schwestern brüder!)
berlin	*role of hugo*	78: grammophon 24193/26509
1931	staatskapelle	lp: preiser LV 206
	zweig	lp: rococo 5293
		lp: top classic BB 45005

zar und zimmermann, excerpt (leb wohl mein flandrisch mädchen!)
berlin	*role of ivanov*	78: grammophon 24193/26509
1931	staatskapelle	lp: dg 88 015
	zweig	lp: preiser LV 206
		lp: rococo 5293
		lp: top classic BB 45005
		lp: gutenberg ASL 1331

PIETRO MASCAGNI (1863-1945)

cavalleria rusticana, excerpt (o lola ch' ai di latti fior di spino)
berlin	*role of turiddu*	78: grammophon 90059
1928	orchestra	45: dg EPL 30 176
	gurlitt	lp: dg 88 015
		lp: preiser LV 1329
		lp: top classic BB 45005

cavalleria rusticana, excerpt (viva il vino!)
berlin	orchestra	78: grammophon 90059
1928	gurlitt	lp: preiser LV 1329
		lp: top classic BB 45005

cavalleria rusticana, excerpt (mamma quel vino e generoso!)
berlin	orchestra	78: grammophon 67205/95233
1928	gurlitt	lp: preiser LV 1329
		lp: top classic BB 45005

HANS MAY (1886-1958)

frag' nicht
berlin	orchestra	78: grammophon 25122
1933	schütze	

ein lied geht um die welt
berlin	orchestra	78: grammophon 25122
1933	schütze	cd: franz-völker-kreis RR 501

ERICH MEYER-HELMUND (1861-1932)

deutschland blühe neu auf! (deutschland sieht aus dunkler nacht)
berlin	staatskapelle	78: grammophon 24806
1932	melichar	

rokoko-ständchen (gute nacht mein holdes süsses mädchen!)
berlin	orchestra	78: grammophon 19730
1927	heidenreich	

das zauberlied (wenn dein ich denk')
berlin	unknown	78: grammophon 27001
1927	pianist	

GIACOMO MEYERBEER (1791-1864)

l' africaine, excerpt (o paradis!)
berlin	*role of vasco*	78: grammophon 95186
1928	orchestra	lp: preiser LV 78
	prüwer	lp: top classic TC 9065
		lp: gutenberg ASL 1331
		cd: preiser 89005

CARL MILLOECKER (1842-1899)

der bettelstudent, excerpt (ich knüpfte manche zarte bande)
berlin	unknown	78: grammophon 19792
1928	orchestra and conductor	cd: preiser 89221
berlin	staatskapelle	grammophon unpublished
28 october 1932	melichar	
berlin	staatskapelle	78: grammophon 10269/10284/48010
20 october 1934	melichar	lp: rococo 5293
		cd: preiser 89221

der bettelstudent. excerpt (ich hab' sie ja nur!)
berlin	staatskapelle	78: grammophon 27068
1928	and chorus snaga	cd: preiser 89221

millöcker **der bettelstudent, excerpt (ich hab' kein geld, bin vogelfrei!)**
berlin	unknown	78: grammophon 19792
1928	orchestra and conductor	cd: preiser 89221

berlin	staatskapelle	78: grammophon 10269
20 october 1934	melichar	cd: preiser 89221

der feldprediger, excerpt (traumwalzer)
berlin	staatskapelle	78: grammophon 24177
1931	melichar	lp: rococo 5293
		cd: preiser 89221

gasparone, excerpt (er soll dein herr sein!)
berlin	orchestra	78: grammophon 22254
1928	gurlitt	cd: preiser 89221

WOLFGANG AMADEUS MOZART (1756-1791)

die zauberflöte, excerpt (dies bildnis ist bezaubernd schön)
berlin	*role of tamino*	78: grammophon 67161
10 february	staatskapelle	lp: top classic TC 9065
1937	f.a.schmidt	lp: preiser LV 1329
		cd: preiser 89070
		another take recorded on 6 february 1937

die zauberflöte, excerpt (wie stark ist nicht dein zauberton)
berlin	staatskapelle	78: grammophon 67161
6 february	f.a.schmidt	lp: top classic TC 9065
1937		lp: historia H 642-643
		lp: preiser LV 1329
		cd: preiser 89070
		another take recorded on 10 february 1937

das veilchen (ein veilchen auf der wiese stand)
berlin	rupp	78: grammophon 23468
1930		cd: preiser 89997

AGUSTIN PEREZ (1846-1907)

ay ay ay!
berlin	orchestra	78: grammophon 19713
1927	heidenreich	*sung to the text schlaf ein mein blond engelein*

berlin	unknown	78: grammophon 15186/19786
1928	orchestra and conductor	*sung to a different text*

JOHANN PETERS

spielmanns lied (und legt ihr zwischen mich und sie auch berg und tal)
berlin	orchestra	78: grammophon 20900/42479
1927	heidenreich	

HANS PFITZNER (1869-1949)

wie frühlingsahnung weht es
berlin	raucheisen	lp: acanta 40.23532
13 november		
1944		

GUSTAV ADOLF PRESSEL (1827-1890)

an der weser (hier hab' ich so manches liebe mal mit meiner laute gesessen)
berlin	orchestra	78: grammophon 19729
1927	heidenreich	

GIACOMO PUCCINI (1858-1924)

tosca, excerpt (recondita armonia)
berlin	*role of*	78: grammophon 90037
1928	*cavaradossi*	78: brunswick DE 7021
	orchestra	lp: preiser LV 1329
	prüwer	lp: dg 88 015
		lp: top classic BB 45005

tosca, excerpt (e lucevan le stelle)
berlin	orchestra	78: grammophon 90037
1928	prüwer	78: brunswick DE 7021
		lp: preiser LV 1329
		lp: gutenberg ASL 1331

NIKOLAI RIMSKY-KORSAKOV (1844-1908)

sadko, excerpt (hindulied)
berlin	staatskapelle	78: grammophon 10270
20 october	melichar	
1934		

CLEMENS SCHMALSTICH (1880-1960)

die sonne hat den rhein geküsst (mein leben gehört nicht meinem süssen liebchen allein)
berlin	paul godwin-	78: grammophon 23316
1930	künstler-	cd: franz-völker-kreis CDFVK 1
	orchester	

FRANZ SCHUBERT (1797-1828)
am meer/schwanengesang
berlin	unknown	78: grammophon 19912
1928	pianist	cd: preiser 89997

an die musik (du holde kunst, in wieviel grauen stunden)
berlin	grossmann	78: grammophon 62836
28 october		cd: preiser 89997
1941		cd: dg 459 0082/459 0662

der atlas/schwanengesang
berlin	unknown	78: grammophon 21653
1928	pianist	cd: preiser 89997

du bist die ruh'
berlin	unknown	78: grammophon 19911
1928	pianist	cd: preiser 89997

der leiermann/winterreise
berlin	unknown	78: grammophon 19912
1928	pianist	cd: preiser 89997

die liebe hat gelogen
berlin	grossmann	78: grammophon 62837
28 october		cd: preiser 89997
1941		

der musensohn (durch feld und wald zu schweifen)
berlin	grossmann	78: grammophon 62837
28 october		cd: preiser 89997
1941		cd: dg 459 0082/459 0662

nacht und träume (heil'ge nacht du sinkest nieder!)
berlin	grossmann	78: grammophon 62836
28 october		cd: preiser 89997
1941		

der neugierige/die schöne müllerin
berlin	unknown	78: grammophon 21653
1928	pianist	cd: preiser 89997

die post/winterreise
berlin	grossmann	78: grammophon 62830
28 october		cd: preiser 89997
1941		

schubert das rosenband (im frühlingsgarten fand ich sie)
berlin grossmann 78: grammophon 62830
28 october cd: preiser 89997
1941

ständchen/schwanengesang
berlin unknown 78: grammophon 19911
1928 pianist cd: preiser 89997

berlin städtische oper unpublished reichsrundfunk broadcast
7 october orchestra
1944 steinkopf

ungeduld/die schöne müllerin
berlin heidenreich 78: grammophon 20899/42478
1927 cd: preiser 89997

das dreimädlerhaus, potpourri from the operetta arranged by berthé from the melodies of schubert
berlin staatskapelle 78: grammophon 24807
1932 melichar

das dreimädlerhaus, excerpt (was schöneres könnt' sein als ein wiener lied)
berlin orchestra 78: grammophon 24651
1931 melichar cd: preiser 89221
 cd: franz-völker-kreis CDFVK 1

1928 recordings of schubert lieder may have had the incorrect label description of orchestral accompaniment

ROBERT SCHUMANN (1810-1856)

die lotosblume/myrten
berlin rupp 78: grammophon 23468
1930 cd: preiser 89997

wanderlied/kerner-lieder
berlin raucheisen 78: grammophon 23084
1929 cd: preiser 89997

BEDRICH SMETANA (1824-1884)

dalibor, excerpt (whose is the spell?)
berlin	staatskapelle	78: grammophon 67603
19 november	steeger	lp: top classic TC 9043
1940		lp: scala (usa) 863
		cd: preiser 89070

JOSEPH SNAGA

serenade (liebchen die am fenster steht)
berlin	orchestra	78: grammophon 21996
1928	gurlitt	

MISCHA SPOLIANSKY (1898-1985)

heute nacht oder nie, from the film das lied einer nacht
berlin	staatskapelle	78: grammophon 24790
1932	melichar	cd: franz-völker-kreis RR 501

ROBERT STOLZ (1880-1975)

dann geh' ich hinaus in den wiener wald (ich geh' durch die strassen)
berlin   orchestra   78: grammophon 24651
1931   melichar   cd: franz-völker-kreis CDFVK 1

im prater blüh'n wieder die bäume (kinder schaut's zum fenster 'raus!)
berlin   orchestra   78: grammophon 15185/19728
1927   heidenreich   lp: marcato 306.142/310.433
                                             cd: franz-völker-kreis CDFVK 1

ob blond oder braun, from the film ich lieb' alle frau'n
berlin   staatskapelle   78: grammophon 10412
1934   melichar   78: decca F 5931
                                            cd: franz-völker-kreis RR 501

schenk' mir dein herz heut' nacht, from the film ich lieb' alle frau'n
berlin   staatskapelle   78: grammophon 10412
1934   melichar   78: decca F 5931

OSCAR STRAUS (1870-1954)

ein walzertraum, excerpt (da draussen im duftenden garten)
berlin   staatskapelle   78: grammophon 22254
1928   snaga

JOHANN STRAUSS (1825-1899)

die fledermaus, abridged operetta on five 78rpm records
berlin   *role of alfred*   78: grammophon 15289-15293/
1929   staatskapelle   95313-95317
            and chorus   cd: pearl GEM 0087
            weigert
            pfahl
            kern
            ruziczka
            klust
            henke
            domgraf-fassbänder
            fleischer-janczak

die fledermaus, excerpt (trinke liebchen trinke schnell!)
berlin   orchestra   78: grammophon 19791/22253
1928   snaga   78: decca PO 5002
            kochhahn   45: dg EPH 21 117
                                      lp: dg 635 067
                                      cd: preiser 89221

die fledermaus, excerpts (im feuerstrom der reben; brüderlein und schwesterlein!)
berlin   staatskapelle   78: grammophon 10017/22173
1928   snaga   cd: preiser 89221
            kochhahn
            bassth
            eisinger
            klust
            henke
            witting
            kandl

eine nacht in venedig, excerpt (komm' in die gondel!)
berlin   orchestra   78: grammophon 10443/21040
1927   heidenreich   cd: preiser 89221

eine nacht in venedig, excerpt (sei mir gegrüsst du holdes venezia!)
berlin   orchestra   78: grammophon 21043
1927   heidenreich   lp: dg 88 015
                                      cd: preiser 89221

j.strauss **eine nacht in venedig, excerpt (treu sein das liegt mir nicht!)**
berlin   orchestra   78: grammophon 21043
1927   heidenreich   cd: preiser 89221

der zigeunerbaron, excerpt (als flotter geist)
berlin   orchestra   78: grammophon 19791
1928   snaga   lp: dg 88 015
                                        cd: austrian radio LC 5130
                                        cd: preiser 89221

der zigeunerbaron, excerpt (werbelied and czardas)
berlin   staatskapelle   78: grammophon 27072
1928   and chorus   lp: dg 88 015
                  snaga   cd: preiser 89221

der zigeunerbaron, excerpt (ha seht es winkt!)
berlin   orchestra   78: grammophon 22253
1929   snaga   cd: preiser 89221
                  kochhahn
                  bassth

der zigeunerbaron, excerpt (mein aug' bewacht!)
berlin   orchestra   78: grammophon 27072
1929   snaga   cd: preiser 89221
                  kochhahn
                  bassth

RICHARD STRAUSS (1864-1949)

die ägyptische helena, fragments (helfet dem weibe ihr unteren dunklen!; die ich zurückliess auf meinem berge; helena oder wie sonst ich dich nenne!)

vienna	*role of menelas*	cd: koch 3-1455-2
20 september	vienna	
1933	philharmonic	
	vienna opera	
	chorus	
	krauss	
	ursuleac	
	bokor	
	jerger	

die ägyptische helena, excerpt (eilig zusammengeraffte gaben!)

vienna	vienna	lp: teletheater 120.747
20 september	philharmonic	cd: koch 3-1455-2
1933	vienna opera	
	chorus	
	krauss	
	ursuleac	
	rosvaenge	
	jerger	

strauss **die frau ohne schatten, excerpt (bleib' und wache, bis sie dich ruft!)**
vienna	*role of kaiser*	cd: koch 3-1466-2
1 june	vienna	
1933	philharmonic	
	krauss	
	rünger	

die frau ohne schatten, excerpt (falke du wiedergefundenee!)
vienna	vienna	lp: ed smith UORC 345
1 june	philharmonic	
1933	krauss	

die frau ohne schatten, excerpt (wenn das herz aus kristall)
vienna	vienna	lp: teletheater 120.747
1 june	philharmonic	cd: koch 3-1466-2
1933	krauss	
	ursuleac	

die frau ohne schatten, excerpt (das sind die nicht geborenen!)
vienna	vienna	cd: koch 3-1466-2
1 june	philharmonic	
1933	krauss	
	ursuleac	

allerseelen (stell' auf den tisch die duftenden reseden)
berlin	rupp	78: grammophon 10305
1 december		cd: preiser 89997
1934		cd: dg 459 0082/459 0662
		dg issue dated 19 november 1934

breit' über mein haupt dein schwarzes haar
berlin	raucheisen	lp: acanta 40.23546
26 october		
1944		

strauss **freundliche vision** (nicht im schlafe hab' ich das geträumt)
berlin steeger 78: grammophon 62817
18-22 cd: preiser 89997
april
1939

berlin raucheisen lp: acanta 40.23546
26 october
1944

ich trage meine minne
berlin steeger grammophon unpublished
18 april
1939

mit deinen blauen augen
frankfurt czernik unpublished radio broadcast
14 august *hessischer rundfunk*
1951

ruhe meine seele (nicht ein lüftchen regt sich leise)
berlin steeger grammophon unpublished
18 april
1939

frankfurt czernik unpublished radio broadcast
14 august *hessischer rundfunk*
1951

strauss sehnsucht (ich ging den weg entlang)
frankfurt	czernik	unpublished radio broadcast
14 august		*hessischer rundfunk*
1951		

ständchen (mach auf doch leise mein kind!)
berlin	unknown	78: grammophon 21652
1928	pianist	cd: preiser 89997
		original issue may have had incorrect label
		description of orchestral accompaniment

zürich	unknown	unpublished private recording
1950	pianist	for hug company

frankfurt	czernik	unpublished radio broadcast
14 august		*hessischer rundfunk*
1951		

traum durch die dämmerung (weite wiesen im dämmergrau)
berlin	steeger	78: grammophon 62817
18-22		cd: preiser 89997
april		cd: dg 459 0082/459 0662
1939		

winterweihe (in diesen wintertagen)
berlin	rupp	78: grammophon 10305
1 december		cd: preiser 89997
1934		

berlin	raucheisen	lp: acanta 40.23546
26 october		
1944		

zueignung (ja du weisst es teure seele!)
berlin	unknown	78: grammophon 21652
1928	pianist	cd: preiser 89997
		original issue may have had incorrect label
		description of orchestral accompaniment

berlin	raucheisen	unpublished reichsrundfunk broadcast
26 october		
1944		

ARTHUR SULLIVAN (1842-1900)

let me dream again
berlin   staatskapelle   78: grammophon 24200
1931   zweig

RICHARD TAUBER (1892-1948)

rot ist dein mund, from the film das lockende ziel
berlin   paul godwin-   78: grammophon 23125
1930   künstler-
                 orchester

es war einmal ein frühlingstraum, from the film das lockende ziel
berlin   paul godwin-   78: grammophon 23125
1930   künstler-   cd: franz-völker-kreis RR 501
                 orchester

ENRICO TOSELLI (1883-1926)

serenata
berlin   unknown   78: grammophon 10449/23467/
1929   orchestra and   23636
                 conductor

GIUSEPPE VERDI (1813-1901)

aida, excerpt (celeste aida)
berlin	*role of radames*	78: grammophon 67159/67205/95377
1930	staatskapelle	45: dg EPL 30 169
	weigert	lp: preiser LV 206
		lp: top classic TC 9065
		cd: preiser 89005
		catalogue number 67159 was subsequently re-used for völker's 1937 recording of no pagliacco non son from i pagliacci

don carlo, excerpt (e mezzanotte!/ed io che tremava al tuo aspetto)
vienna	*role of carlo*	cd: koch 3-1466-2
25 february	vienna	
1933	philharmonic	
	krauss	
	rünger	
	schipper	

don carlo, excerpt (tu piu figlio non h'ai!)
vienna	vienna	lp: ed smith EJS 334
16 december	philharmonic	
1936	walter	
	kipnis	
	jerger	

don carlo, excerpt (vago sogno m' arrise!/il duolo della terra)
vienna	vienna	lp: ed smith EJS 334
16 december	philharmonic	lp: teletheater 76.23589
1936	vienna opera	cd: koch 3-1460-2
	chorus	
	walter	
	konetzni	
	kipnis	
	alsen	
	jerger	

la forza del destino, excerpt (o tu che in seno agli angeli)
berlin	*role of alvaro*	grammophon unpublished
25 october	staatskapelle	*two different takes were recorded*
1937	schüler	

verdi **otello, excerpt (esultate!)**

munich	*role of otello*	cd: preiser 90364
24 february	bavarian state	
1946	orchestra	
	and chorus	
	wetzelsberger	

otello, excerpt (gia della notte densa)

vienna	vienna	cd: koch 3-1466-2
15 december	philharmonic	*recording incomplete*
1933	krauss	
	ursuleac	

munich	bavarian state	cd: preiser 90364
24 february	orchestra	
1946	wetzelsberger	
	cunitz	

otello, excerpt (tu indietro?)

vienna	vienna	lp: teletheater 120.841
15 december	philharmonic	cd: koch 3-1466-2
1933	krauss	*this version begins earlier at desdemona real*
	manowarda	

berlin	staatskapelle	78: grammophon 62776
7 october	schüler	45: dg EPL 30 162
1937		lp: preiser LV 1329
		cd: preiser 89070/90364
		cd: dg 459 0052/459 0662

verdi otello, excerpt (era la notte/talor vedeste in mano di desdemona)
vienna	vienna	cd: koch 3-1466-2
15 december	philharmonic	
1933	krauss	
	manowarda	

otello, excerpt (dio mi potevi)
berlin	städtische oper	lp: acanta 98.221776
7 october	orchestra	
1944	steinkopf	

munich	bavarian state	cd: preiser 90364
24 february	orchestra	
1946	wetzelsberger	

otello, excerpt (cassio e la!)
munich	bavarian state	cd: preiser 90364
24 february	orchestra	
1946	wetzelsberger	
	klarwein	
	hotter	

otello, excerpt (nium mi tema)
berlin	staatskapelle	78: grammophon 27325/67159/95494
1930	weigert	lp: preiser LV 78
		lp: gutenberg ASL 1331
		cd: preiser 89005/90364

rigoletto, excerpt (questa o quella!)
berlin	*role of duke*	78: grammophon 90058
1928	orchestra	45: dg EPL 30 176
	prüwer	lp: dg 88 015
		lp: preiser LV 1329
		lp: top classic TC 9065

rigoletto, excerpt (la donna e mobile!)
berlin	orchestra	78: grammophon 90056
1928	gurlitt	45: dg EPL 30 176
		lp: dg 88 015
		lp: preiser LV 1329
		lp: top classic BB 45005

verdi **il trovatore, abridged opera on four 78rpm records**
berlin	*role of manrico*	78: grammophon 15277-15280/
1929	staatskapelle	59084-59087/95260-95263
	and chorus	*excerpts*
	weigert	78: grammophon 27334/57021
	toros	
	klust	
	dörwald	
	weltner	
	henke	
	fleischer-janczak	

il trovatore, excerpt (ah si ben mio)
berlin	orchestra	78: grammophon 67205/95186
1928	gurlitt	lp: gutenberg ASL 1331
		lp: preiser LV 78/LV 1329
		cd: preiser 89005

il trovatore, excerpt (di quella pira!)
berlin	staatskapelle	78: grammophon 24240/62776
1931	zweig	45: dg EPL 30 162
		lp: preiser LV 206
		lp: top classic BB 45005
		lp: tap records T 133
		cd: bongiovanni GB 10512

RICHARD WAGNER (1813-1883)

der fliegende holländer
bayreuth	*role of erik*	cd: preiser 90232
18 july	bayreuth	*excerpts*
1942	festival	lp: acanta 40.23502
	orchestra	cd: preiser 90364
	and chorus	cd: hamburger archiv für gesangskunst
	kraus	WAGNER 2
	müller	
	asmus	
	berglund	
	hofmann	

der fliegende holländer, excerpt (auf hohem felsen)
berlin	staatskapelle	78: grammophon 67799
1941	steeger	45: dg EPL 30 543
	langhammer	lp: top classic TC 9065
		cd: preiser 89070/89403

der fliegende holländer, excerpt (willst jenes tags du nicht dich mehr entsinnen)
berlin	orchestra	78: grammophon 90051
1928	prüwer	45: dg EPL 30 543
		lp: gutenberg ASL 1331
		lp: emi 1C181 30669-30678M
		cd: musica memoria 30283
		cd: preiser 89005

der fliegende holländer, excerpt (mit gewitter und sturm)
berlin	*role of*	78: grammophon 67208/95233
1928	*steuermann*	78: brunswick 90301
	orchestra	lp: top classic TC 9043
	gurlitt	lp: preiser LV 1329
		lp: scala (usa) 863

158

wagner **lohengrin**

berlin	*role of*	lp: preiser LOH 1-4
31 october	*lohengrin*	cd: preiser 90043
1943	staatskapelle	*excerpts*
	and chorus	lp: acanta DE 21996/DE 23112-23113/
	heger	40.23502/98.221776/HB 22.8630
	müller	cd: hamburger archiv für gesangskunst
	klose	HAGHOF 2/HAGWAGNER 3
	hofmann	cd: preiser 89235/90364
	prohaska	
	grossmann	

lohengrin, excerpt (mein herr und gott!)

bayreuth	bayreuth	78: telefunken SKB 02050
24 august	festival	78: grammophon NSKB 2050
1936	orchestra	lp: telefunken HT 1/KT 11017/642.019
	and chorus	lp: emi 1C181 30669-30678M
	tietjen	cd: teldec 9031 764422
	müller	cd: victoria 290.242
	klose	
	manowarda	
	prohaska	

lohengrin, fragmentary excerpts from act one (nun sei bedankt, mein lieber schwan!/elsa ich liebe dich!/durch gottes sieg ist jetzt dein leben mein!)

vienna	vienna	cd: koch 3-1468-2
19 june	philharmonic	*guest performance by forces of the berlin*
1938	vienna opera	*staatsoper*
	chorus	
	berlin staatsoper	
	chorus	
	tietjen	
	müller	
	klose	
	manowarda	
	prohaska	

wagner **lohengrin, fragmentary excerpts from act one (nun sei bedankt, mein lieber schwan!/du kündest nun dein wahr' gesicht)**

vienna	vienna	cd: koch 3-1466-2
3 june	philharmonic	
1933	vienna opera	
	chorus	
	rühlmann	
	zika	
	rünger	
	manowarda	
	schipper	

lohengrin, excerpt (elsa erhebe dich!)

vienna	vienna	cd: koch 3-1466-2
3 june	philharmonic	
1933	vienna opera	
	chorus	
	rühlmann	
	zika	
	schipper	

vienna	vienna	cd: koch 3-1468-2
19 june	philharmonic	*guest performance by forces of the berlin staatsoper*
1938	vienna opera	
	chorus	
	berlin staatsoper	
	chorus	
	tietjen	
	müller	

wagner **lohengrin, excerpt (das süsse lied verhallt)**

bayreuth 19 july 1936	bayreuth festival orchestra furtwängler müller	lp: ed smith EJS 399 lp: cetra FE 25 lp: acanta HB 22.8630/40.23502/ 40.23520 cd: acanta 44.1055 cd: pilz CD 74807 cd: grammofono AB 78515 cd: iron needle IN 1634-1635 *original recordings begins with radio announcement, act three prelude and treulich geführt*
bayreuth 20 august 1936	bayreuth festival orchestra tietjen müller	78: telefunken SKB 02052 78: ultraphon H 22627 lp: telefunken HT 1/KT 11017/642.019 lp: preiser LV 81 cd: teldec 9031 764422/3984 269192 cd: musica memoria 30.283-284 cd: malibran CDRG 109 *3984 269192 is dated 29 august 1936*
berlin 15 december 1944	berlin radio orchestra rother lemnitz	lp: urania URLP 7019 lp: classics club X 122 lp: acanta 22.221105/98.221776 lp: eterna 820.891/821.873 lp: rca victor RL 30439 cd: pilz CD 87007 cd: minerva MNA 21 cd: radio years RY 76 cd: voce della luna 20002 cd: berlin classics BC 90142 cd: hamburger archiv für gesangskunst HAGLEM 3 *some editions are dated 1943*

wagner **lohengrin, excerpt (atmest du nicht mit mir die süssen düfte?)**
berlin	orchestra	78: grammophon 90051
1928	gurlitt	45: dg EPL 30 545
		lp: preiser LV 10/LV 206
		cd: preiser 89005/89999/90953

lohengrin, excerpt (höchstes vertrau'n hast du schon mir zu danken)
berlin	orchestra	78: grammophon 19711
1927	heidenreich	lp: preiser LV 206
		cd: preiser 89005

bayreuth	bayreuth	78: telefunken SKB 02053
29 august	festival	78: grammophon NSKB 2053
1936	orchestra	78: ultraphon H 22628
	tietjen	lp: telefunken HT 1/KT 11017/642.019
		cd: teldec 9031 764422
		cd: malibran CDRG 109

berlin	berlin radio	lp: urania URLP 7019
15 december	orchestra	lp: classics club X 122
1944	rother	lp: acanta 22.221·105
		lp: eterna 820.891/821.873
		cd: pilz CD 78007
		cd: berlin classics BC 90142
		some editions are dated 1943

lohengrin, fragmentary excerpts from act three (wie hehr erkenn' ich unsrer liebe wesen/sie vor den könig zu geleiten/wollt' ich dem dienst des reinen herzens/seht da den herzog von brabant!)
vienna	vienna	cd: koch 3-1468-2
19 june	philharmonic	*guest performance by forces of the berlin*
1938	vienna opera	*staatsoper*
	chorus	
	berlin staatsoper	
	chorus	
	tietjen	
	müller	
	klose	
	manowarda	

wagner **lohengrin, excerpt (in fernem land)**

berlin 1927	orchestra heidenreich	78: grammophon 19711 45: dg EPL 30 162 lp: dg 2700 703 lp: preiser LV 206 cd: preiser 89005 *2700 703 incorrectly dated 1937*
berlin 1928	unknown orchestra and conductor	78: grammophon 67148/95038 78: supraphon 19711 lp: dg 2721 110/410 8541
bayreuth 19 july 1936	bayreuth festival orchestra furtwängler	lp: ed smith EJS 399 lp: cetra FE 25 lp: acanta 40.23502/40.23520 cd: acanta 40.1055 cd: pilz CD 74807 cd: grammofono AB 78515 cd: iron needle IN 1364-1365
bayreuth 20 august 1936	bayreuth festival orchestra tietjen	78: telefunken SKB 02047/SKB 02049 78: grammophon NSKB 2047/NSKB 2049 78: supraphon H 22622 78: ultraphon H 22622 lp: telefunken UV 241/HT 1/KT 11017/ 642.019 lp: scala (usa) 863 lp: top classic TC 9043 lp: dg 2721 062 cd: musica memoria 30283-30284 cd: memoir classics CDMOIR 405 cd: teldec 9031 764422 cd: malibran CDRG 109 *SKB 02049 and NSKB 02049, and subsequent is on scala, telefunken, top classic, musica memoria, teldec and malibran also contain a second verse (nun höre noch...) which had been deleted by the composer*

wagner lohengrin, excerpt (mein lieber schwan)

berlin 1927	orchestra heidenreich	78: grammophon 19731/67148 78: decca LY 6080 45: dg EPL 30 162 lp: dg 2811 010/410 8541 lp: preiser LV 206 lp: top classic BB 45005 lp: emi EX 29 01693 cd: preiser 89005 cd: documents LV 923-924 cd: vocal archives VA 1148-1149
bayreuth 19 july 1936	bayreuth festival orchestra furtwängler	lp: ed smith EJS 399 lp: cetra FE 25 lp: acanta 40.23520 cd: acanta 40.1055 cd: pilz CD 74807 cd: grammofono AB 78515 cd: iron needle IN 1364-1365
bayreuth 29 august 1936	bayreuth festival orchestra tietjen	78: telefunken SKB 02053 78: grammophon NSKB 2053 78: ultraphon H 22628 78: supraphon H 22628 lp: telefunken HT 1/KT 11017/642.019 lp: scala (usa) 863 lp: fonic 75001 cd: teldec 9031 764422 cd: victoria 290.242 cd: musica memoria 30283-30284 cd: malibran CDRG 109
berlin 15 december 1944	berlin radio orchestra rother	lp: acanta 98.221776

1936 bayreuth festival extracts from lohengrin recorded by telefunken were published simultaneously by that company and by grammophon, völker being an exclusive grammophon recording artist

wagner **die meistersinger von nürnberg, excerpt (am stillen herd)**
berlin	*role of*	78: grammophon 67102/95038
1928	*stolzing*	45: dg EPL 30 543
	orchestra	lp: preiser LV 206
	gurlitt	lp: top classic TC 9065
		cd: preiser 89005

die meistersinger von nürnberg, excerpt (fanget an! so rief der lenz in den wald)
berlin	orchestra	78: grammophon 95161
1928	gurlitt	45: dg EPL 30 543
		lp: preiser LV 206
		lp: top classic TC 9043
		lp: gutenberg ASL 1331
		cd: preiser 89005

die meistersinger von nürnberg, excerpt (morgenlich leuchtend)
berlin	orchestra	78: grammophon 35006/67102/95161
1928	gurlitt	45: dg EPL 30 543
		lp: preiser LV 206
		lp: top classic TC 9065
		lp: gutenberg ASL 1331
		cd: preiser 89005/89229

die meistersinger von nürnberg, excerpt (selig wie die sonne)
vienna	vienna	cd: koch 3-1460-2
13 april	philharmonic	
1934	krauss	
	ursuleac	
	szantho	
	zimmermann	
	jerger	

die meistersinger von nürnberg, fragmentary excerpts from acts two and three (o eva schlimmes weib!/mein freund in holder jugendzeit/zeuge am ort fahret fort!)
vienna	vienna	cd: koch 3-1460-2
13 april	philharmonic	
1934	krauss	
	ursuleac	
	szantho	
	jerger	

wagner rienzi, excerpt (erstehe hohe roma neu!)

vienna	*role of rienzi*	lp: teletheater 120.747
15 may	vienna	cd: koch 3-1450-2/3-1466-2
1933	philharmonic	
	vienna opera	
	chorus	
	krips	
berlin	staatskapelle	78: grammophon 27325/67100/
1933	and chorus	67208/95491
	melichar	45: dg EPL 30 545
		lp: preiser LV 78
		lp: top classic TC 9043
		lp: scala (usa) 863
		lp: gutenberg ASL 1331
		cd: preiser 89005
		cd: musica memoria 30283-30284

rienzi, excerpt (allmächt'ger vater blick' herab!)

berlin	staatskapelle	78: grammophon 67100/95377/95491
1930	weigert	78: brunswick 90380
		lp: preiser LV 78
		lp; top classic TC 9065
		lp: scala (usa) 863
		lp: gutenberg ASL 1331
		cd: musica memoria 30283-30284
		cd: preiser 89005
		cd: nimbus NI 7848
		cd: dg 459 0062/459 0662
		nimbus names conductor as melichar
vienna	vienna	cd: koch 3-1466-2
15 may	philharmonic	
1933	krips	
berlin	staatskapelle	78: grammophon 67799
1941	steeger	lp: frankfurt opera 3A-4265A
		cd: preiser 89070

wagner **rienzi, fragmentary excerpts (dir preis und deiner hohen macht!/
o lass der gnade himmelslicht/der tag ist da!/eh' du von neuem mich
bewegst/heil roma dir! du hast gesiegt!)**
vienna	vienna	cd: koch 3-1466-2
15 may	philharmonic	
1933	vienna opera	
	chorus	
	krips	
	anday	
	gallos	
	ettl	

tannhäuser, excerpt (stets soll nur dir mein lied ertönen)
berlin	staatskapelle	78: grammophon 24240
1930	weigert	45: dg EPL 30 545
		lp: preiser LV 78
		cd: musica memoria 30283-30284

tannhäuser, excerpt (inbrunst im herzen)
berlin	staatskapelle	78: grammophon 27306/67141/95483
1933	melichar	lp: preiser LV 78
		lp: top classic TC 9065
		lp: gutenberg ASL 1331
		cd: preiser 89070

wagner die walküre

bayreuth	*role of siegmund*	unpublished reichsrundfunk broadcast
6 august	bayreuth	*fragments of the broadcast were published on lp by*
1934	festival	*ed smith UORC 264 but did not include the role of*
	orchestra	*siegmund*
	elmendorff	
	leider	
	müller	
	onegin	
	bockelmann	
	manowarda	

die walküre, act one

munich	bavarian state	lp: orfeo S120 842I
7 may	orchestra	cd: orfeo C019 991Z
1947	solti	
	schech	
	dalberg	

die walküre, fragment (wes herd dies auch sei, hier muss ich rasten/labung biet' ich dem lechzenden gaumen)

vienna	vienna	cd: koch 3-1470-2
13 february	philharmonic	*labung biet' ich only*
1936	furtwängler	lp: ed smith EJS 451
	müller	
bayreuth	bayreuth	lp: acanta HB 22.8630/40.23502
17 june	festival	cd: hamburger archiv für gesangskunst
1941	orchestra	HAGWAGNER 5
	tietjen	
	müller	

die walküre, fragment (wasser wie du gewollt/kühlende labung gab mir der quell)

vienna	vienna	cd: koch 3-1462-2
14 september	philharmonic	
1933	krauss	
	lehmann	

die walküre, fragment (friedmund darf ich nicht heissen)

bayreuth	bayreuth	lp: acanta 40.23502
17 june	festival	cd: hamburger archiv für gesangskunst
1941	orchestra	HAGWAGNER 5
	tietjen	

wagner **die walküre, fragment (weither traun kamst du des wegs/auf der leiche lag sie tot)**
vienna   vienna   cd: koch 3-1470-2
13 february   philharmonic
1936   furtwängler
                 müller
                 jerger

die walküre, fragment (feige nur fürchten den, der waffenlos einsam fährt)
vienna   vienna   cd: koch 3-1464-2
11 june   philharmonic
1933   krauss
                 hüni-mihacsek
                 mayr

die walküre, fragment (ich bin's! höre mich an!)
vienna   vienna   cd: koch 3-1470-2
13 february   philharmonic
1936   furtwängler
                 müller

die walküre, excerpt (ein schwert verhiess mir der vater)
berlin   staatskapelle   78: grammophon 27291
1932   melichar   78: brunswick 90312
                                   lp: top classic TC 9043
                                   lp: preiser LV 1329

vienna   vienna   cd: koch 3-1464-2
11 june   philharmonic
1933   krauss

bayreuth   bayreuth   telefunken unpublished
1936   festival   *matrix damaged*
                 orchestra
                 tietjen

berlin   staatskapelle   78: grammophon 67142/95493/566191
25 october   schüler   lp: preiser LV 1329
1937   cd: preiser 89070

wagner **die walküre, excerpt (winterstürme wichen dem wonnemond)**

berlin	orchestra	78: grammophon 19731
1927	heidenreich	78: decca LY 6080

vienna	vienna	lp: teletheater 120.747
1 march	philharmonic	cd: koch 3-1466-2
1933	krauss	*teletheater included brief fragments before and after this extract*

vienna	vienna	cd: koch 3-1464-2
11 june	philharmonic	
1933	krauss	

bayreuth	bayreuth	78: telefunken SKB 02048
24 august	festival	78: grammophon NSKB 2048
1936	orchestra	78: ultraphon H 22623
	tietjen	78: supraphon H 22623
		lp: telefunken HT 11/KT 11017
		lp: top classic TC 9043
		lp: dg 410 8541
		cd: teldec 9031 764422
		cd: musica memoria 30285-30286
		cd: malibran CDRG 109
		cd: preiser 89235

berlin	staatskapelle	78: grammophon 67142/95493/566191
25 october	schüler	45: dg EPL 30 545
1937		lp: preiser LV 1329
		cd: preiser 89070/89404

die walküre, excerpt (was im busen ich barg/o süsseste wonne seligstes weib!)

vienna	vienna	cd: koch 3-1464-2
11 june	philharmonic	
1933	krauss	
	hüni-mihacsek	

bayreuth	bayreuth	78: telefunken SKB 02048
24 august	festival	78: grammophon NSKB 2048
1936	orchestra	78: ultraphon H 22623
	tietjen	78: supraphon H 22623
	müller	lp: telefunken HT 11/KT 11017
		lp: top classic TC 9043
		lp: dg 410 8541
		cd: teldec 9031 764422
		cd: musica memoria 30285-30286
		cd: malibran CDRG 109
		cd: preiser 89235

wagner **die walküre, excerpt** (**o lass in nähe zu dir mich neigen!/im lenzesmond leuchtest du hell**)

bayreuth 24 august 1936	bayreuth festival orchestra tietjen müller	78: telefunken SKB 02048 78: grammophon NSKB 2048 78: ultraphon H 22623 78: supraphon H 22623 lp: telefunken HT 11/KT 11017 lp: top classic TC 9043 lp: dg 410 8541 cd: teldec 9031 764422 cd: musica memoria 30285-30286 cd: malibran CDRG 109
vienna 13 october 1936	vienna philharmonic walter konetzni	cd: koch 3-1459-2

die walküre, fragment (**ein minnetraum gemahnt auch mich**)

vienna 13 february 1936	vienna philharmonic furtwängler müller	cd: koch 3-1470-2
bayreuth 24 august 1936	bayreuth festival orchestra tietjen müller	78: telefunken SKB 02048 78: grammophon NSKB 2048 78: ultraphon H 22623 78: supraphon H 22623 lp: telefunken HT 11/KT 11017 lp: top classic TC 9043 lp: dg 410 8541 cd: teldec 9031 764422 cd: musica memoria 30285-30286 cd: malibran CDRG 109

wagner **die walküre, excerpt (siegmund heiss' ich und siegmund bin ich!.....to end of act one)**

berlin 1932	staatskapelle melichar	78: grammophon 27291 78: brunswick 90312 lp: preiser LV 1329
vienna 14 september 1933	vienna philharmonic krauss lehmann	cd: koch 3-1462-2
vienna 1 november 1934	vienna philharmonic krauss ursuleac	cd: koch 3-1466-2
bayreuth 24 august 1936	bayreuth festival orchestra tietjen müller	78: telefunken SKB 02047 78: grammophon NSKB 2042 78: ultraphon H 22622 78: supraphon H 26622 lp: telefunken HT 11/KT 11017 lp: scala (usa) 863 lp: dg 410 8541 cd: teldec 9031 764422 cd: malibran CDRG 109
vienna 13 october 1936	vienna philharmonic walter konetzni	cd: koch 3-1459-2

1936 bayreuth festival extracts from act one of walküre recorded by telefunken were published simultaneously by that company and by grammophon, völker being an exclusive grammophon recording artist

wagner **die walküre, fragment (raste nun hier, gönne dir ruh'!)**
vienna   vienna   lp: legato LCD 139
14 september   philharmonic   cd: koch 3-1462-2
1933   krauss
                    lehmann

die walküre, fragment (verweile süssestes weib!)
vienna   vienna   cd: koch 3-1470-2
13 february   philharmonic
1936   furtwängler
                    müller

die walküre, fragment (ruhe nun aus, rede zu mir!)
vienna   vienna   cd: koch 3-1459-2
13 october   philharmonic
1936   walter
                    konetzni

wagner **die walküre, fragments** (der dir nun folgt, wohin führst du den helden?/kennst du das schwert?)

vienna	vienna	cd: koch 3-1464-2
11 june	philharmonic	
1933	krauss	
	jeritza	

die walküre, fragment (muss ich denn fallen, nicht fahr' ich nach walhall!)

vienna	vienna	cd: koch 3-1470-2
13 february	philharmonic	
1936	furtwängler	
	a.konetzni	

die walküre, fragment (so jung und schön erschimmerst du mir)

vienna	vienna	cd: koch 3-1459-2
13 october	philharmonic	
1936	walter	
	merker	

die walküre, fragment (zauberfest bezähmt ein schlaf)

vienna	vienna	cd: koch 3-1466-2
1 november	philharmonic	
1934	krauss	
	ursuleac	

die walküre, fragment (drohst du mit frauen, so ficht nun selber!)

vienna	vienna	cd: koch 3-1459-2
13 octoner	philharmonic	
1935	walter	
	konetzni	
	merker	
	hofmann	

CARL MARIA VON WEBER (1786-1826)

der freischütz, excerpt (o diese sonne!)

vienna 10 may 1933	*role of max* vienna philharmonic vienna opera chorus krips ettl manowarda	cd: koch 3-1453-2
salzburg 3 august 1939	vienna philharmonic vienna opera chorus knappertsbusch bisutti bohnen franter	cd: radio years RY 70 cd: koch 3-1467-2

der freischütz, excerpt (nein länger trag' ich nicht die qualen/durch die wälder, durch die auen!)

berlin 1927	orchestra heidenreich	78: grammophon 19683 lp: preiser LV 206 lp: kurier ZK 100.101
berlin 28 october 1932	staatskapelle melichar	grammophon unpublished *test pressing of durch die wälder only*
vienna 10 may 1933	vienna philharmonic krips	lp: ed smith EJS 332 cd: koch 3-1453-2
berlin 1938	staatskapelle steeger	78: grammophon 67260 lp: preiser LV 1329 lp: top classic TC 9043 cd: preiser 89070

weber der freischütz, excerpt (hier im ird'schen jammertal)
vienna	vienna	cd: koch 3-1453
10 may	philharmonic	
1933	krips	
	manowarda	

salzburg	vienna	cd: radio years RY 70
3 august	philharmonic	cd: koch 3-1467-2
1939	knappertsbusch	
	bohnen	

der freischütz, excerpt (wehe! die wilde jagd!)
salzburg	vienna	cd: radio years RY 70
3 august	philharmonic	cd: koch 3-1467-2
1939	vienna opera chorus	
	knappertsbusch	
	bohnen	
	soetber	

FELIX VON WEINGARTNER (1863-1942)

liebesfeier (an ihren bunten liedern klettert die lerche)
berlin	orchestra	78: grammophon 20898
1927	heidenreich	

HUGO WOLF (1860-1903)

gesang weylas, arranged by steinkopf
berlin	städtische oper	unpublished reichsrundfunk broadcast
7 october	orchestra	
1944	steinkopf	

heimweh/eichendorff-lieder
berlin	heidenreich	78: grammophon 20899
1927		cd: preiser 89997

CARL ZELLER (1842-1898)

der kellermeister, excerpt (lass' dir zeit!)
berlin	orchestra	78: grammophon 19908/57441
1928	gurlitt	cd: preiser 89221

der vogelhändler, excerpt (wie mein ahn'l zwanzig jahr')
berlin	orchestra	78: grammophon 19908
1928	gurlitt	cd: preiser 89221

der vogelhändler, excerpt (schenkt man sich rosen im tirol)
berlin	staatskapelle	78: grammophon 15182/27068/57414/
1928	and chorus	57441/566304
	snaga	lp: rococo 5293
		cd: preiser 89221
		57414 did not name völker on label

MISCELLANEOUS POPULAR SONGS

ach so ein zarter liebestraum
berlin orchestra 78: grammophon 25064/47114
1931 melichar

allein kann man nicht glücklich sein
berlin orchestra 78: grammophon 25323
1932 schütze

am rhein und beim wein (mit rheinwein füllt den becher!)
berlin orchestra 78: grammophon 19682
1927 heidenreich

an deinem herzen lass mich träumen
berlin staatskapelle 78: grammophon 23917/47115
1931 zweig

denn im blühenden lachenden moseltal (wo der rebensaft spendet)
berlin paul godwin- 78: grammophon 23317
1930 künstler-
orchester

drunt' in der lobau (wo die donau mit silbernen armen)
berlin orchestra 78: grammophon 47064
1 october schütze lp: rococo 5293
1936 cd: franz-völker-kreis CDFVK 1

einmal sagt man sich adieu, from the film die wunderbare lüge der nina petrowa
berlin unknown 78: grammophon 22644
1929 orchestra and cd: franz-völker-kreis RR 501
conductor

es gibt eine frau, die dich niemals vergisst (frauen gibt es hunderte, geliebte und bewunderte)
berlin gurlitt *first version*
1929 78: grammophon 22240
second version
78: grammophon 22240/25092

es gibt nur eine melodie
berlin orchestra 78: grammophon 25323
1933 schütze

emigrant (übers meer möcht' ich fliehen!)
berlin staatskapelle 78: grammophon 10603/25200
1932 melichar

fahr' wohl! (es dämmert in den fahlen bäumen)
berlin orchestra 78: grammophon 19712
1927 heidenreich

frühling zog ein (was strahlet nur so freudehell die sonne?)
berlin orchestra 78: grammophon 20898
1927 heidenreich

gib' nur acht, über nacht kommt die liebe!
berlin paul godwin- 78: grammophon 23467
1930 künstler-
 orchester

gruss an marburg (marburg dir gilt unser grüssen)
berlin orchestra 78: grammophon 19740
1927 heidenreich

grüss' mir das blonde kind vom rhein (ich wand're in die weite welt)
berlin orchestra 78: grammophon 21042
1927 heidenreich

des hegansängers gruss an die heimat (seid mir gegrüsst im sonnenglanz!)
berlin	unknown	78: grammophon 22737
1929	orchestra and conductor	cd: franz-völker-kreis CDFVK 1

ich bin verliebt in meine eigene frau (junggesell' nicht so schnell!)
berlin	unknown	78: grammophon 22709
1929	orchestra and conductor	cd: franz-völker-kreis RR 501

ich hab' dich lieb (hab' die welt bereist)
berlin	unknown	78: grammophon 22710
1929	orchestra and conductor	

ich hab' heut' nacht vom rhein geträumt (wir haben manches fläschchen heut' vergossen)
berlin	orchestra	78: grammophon 21044
1927	heidenreich	cd: franz-völker-kreis CDFVK 1

heut' ist ja noch heut' (es kommt eine zeit)
berlin	orchestra	78: grammophon 10603/24490
1930	melichar	

ich küsse deine lippen
berlin	unknown	78: grammophon 19789
1928	orchestra and conductor	

im rolandsbogen (ich kam von fern gezogen)
berlin	orchestra	78: grammophon 19727
1927	heidenreich	cd: franz-völker-kreis CDFVK 1

in der pfalz (heute nacht noch vor dem ersten hahnenschrei)
berlin	orchestra	78: grammophon 19702
1927	heidenreich	cd: franz-völker-kreis CDFVK 1

kam von schwarzwalds bergen
berlin	paul godwin-	78: grammophon 23318
1930	künstler-orchester	cd: franz-völker-kreis CDFVK 1

keine frau kann schöner sein (blau wie der südseehimmel)
berlin   unknown   78: grammophon 23838
1931   orchestra and   cd: franz-völker-kreis RR 501
                conductor

komm' mit mir ins reich der träume (in dunkler nacht, wenn niemand wacht)
berlin   staatskapelle   78: grammophon 23917
1931   zweig

ja wenn mein mädel hochzeit hat
berlin   orchestra   78: grammophon 25359
1932   schütze

lieblicher goldener moselwein! (mein weg ging dahin in die blühende welt)
berlin   paul godwin-   78: grammophon 23317
1930   künstler-
                orchester

das lied der liebe hat eine süsse melodie (lieder gibt es viele auf der welt)
berlin   paul godwin-   78: grammophon 22645
1929   künstler-
                orchester

mädel bin ich dir so gut (am rhein wo im glase der goldene wein)
berlin	unknown	78: grammophon 19789
1928	orchestra and conductor	

manon (dunkle zypressen, sie schaukeln im winde)
berlin	unknown	78: grammophon 21877/23636
1928	orchestra and conductor	

märchen der liebe (so wie ein märchen ist uns're liebe)
berlin	unknown	78: grammophon 47186
1937	orchestra and conductor	cd: franz-völker-kreis RR 501

mein heimatland, o du herrlicher rhein!
berlin	orchestra	78: grammophon 20900/211061
1927	heidenreich	

mein lied (im silbernen mondlicht)
berlin	orchestra	78: grammophon 24490/47115
1931	melichar	

mein kleines liebeslied (wenn die lagune still im abendschimmer liegt)
berlin	unkown	78: grammophon 47186
1937	orchestra and conductor	cd: franz-völker-kreis RR 501

mein süsses lieb mir träumte
berlin	orchestra	78: grammophon 19712
1927	heidenreich	

nach freiburg zieht mein herz mich
berlin	paul godwin-künstler-orchester	78: grammophon 23318
1930		cd: franz-völker-kreis CDFVK 1

noch sind die tage der rosen (noch ist die schöne goldene zeit)
berlin   unknown   78: grammophon 10780/22738
1929   orchestra and
                  conductor

o heimat mein! (ein tiefes sehnen füllt die brust)
berlin   orchestra   78: grammophon 19713
1927   heidenreich

öffne dein herz meiner liebe, from the film die stimme des herzens
berlin   unknown   78: grammophon 47095
1937   orchestra and
                  conductor

opern-potpourri
berlin   orchestra   78: grammophon 24345
1931   melichar   78: decca PO 5001

pfälzerlied (am deutschen strom am grünen rhein)
berlin   orchestra   78: grammophon 10799/21106
1927   heidenreich

ein rheinisches mädchen bei rheinischem wein (hast du geliebt am schönen rhein)
berlin   orchestra   78: grammophon 10799/21042
1927   heidenreich   cd: franz-völker-kreis CDFVK 1

rheinlandmädel (war einstens der herrgott)
berlin   unknown   78: grammophon 10799/22710
1928   orchestra and
                  conductor

schönau mein paradies
berlin	orchestra	78: grammophon 24419/47113
1931	melichar	78: decca PO 5022
		cd: franz-völker-kreis CDFVK 1

der schönste augenblick (schön ist's wenn zwei sterne)
berlin	unknown	78: grammophon 21934
1928	orchestra and conductor	

sei gegrüsst du mein schönes sorrent! (wie die tage so golden verfliessen)
berlin	gurlitt	78: grammophon 15185/27151
1929		

serenata veneziana, from the film vergissmeinnicht
berlin	staatskapelle	78: grammophon 10411
4 september	melichar	78: decca F 5930
1935		cd: franz-völker-kreis RR 501

die sieger
zürich	unnamed	unpublished private recording for
1950	pianist	hug company

stolzenfels am rhein (ein grenadier auf dem dorfplatz stand)
berlin	unknown	78: grammophon 24617
1929	orchestra and conductor	cd: franz-völker-kreis CDFVK 1

tango classique (die nacht steigt)
berlin	unknown	78: grammophon 24371
1931	orchestra and conductor	45: dg EPH 21 117

tausend sterne leuchten in der blauen frühlingsnacht
berlin	orchestra	78: grammophon 25324
1933	schütze	

der trompeter (wenn dieser siegesmarsch in das ohr nur schallt)
berlin   orchestra   78: grammophon 19702
1927   heidenreich

vergissmeinnicht, from the film of the same name
berlin   staatskapelle   78: grammophon 10411
4 march   melichar   78: decca F 5930
1935   cd: franz-völker-kreis RR 501

volkslieder-potpourri
berlin   orchestra   78: grammophon 24444
1931   melichar

vom rhein der wein (was bringen uns die reben?)
berlin   orchestra   78: grammophon 21044
1927   heidenreich

von wien durch die welt/operetten-potpourri
berlin   staatskapelle   78: grammophon 24939
1932   melichar

was du fragen willst
berlin   unknown   78: grammophon 24371
1931   orchestra and
                   conductor

was ist wein? (fröhlicher bursche wandert am rhein)
berlin unknown 78: grammophon 21248
1928 orchestra and
  conductor

wenn die alten bäume rauschen
berlin orchestra 78: grammophon 25359
1933 schütze

wenn die liebe singt/operetten-potpourri
berlin staatskapelle 78: grammophon 27346/35079
1937 marszalek

wenn man verliebt ist (schöne frau das geschick ist mir gnädig!)
berlin unknown 78: grammophon 22645
1929 orchestra and
  conductor

wiener fiakerlied (ich führ' zwa harbe rappen!)
berlin orchestra 78: grammophon 19728
1927 heidenreich cd: franz-völker-kreis CDFVK 1

winterlied (komm' aus der engen stadt)
berlin unnamed 78: grammophon 21651
1928 pianist *described on label as orchestral accompaniment*

des zechers lust am rhein (hab' draussen mich herumgetrieben)
berlin orchestra 78: grammophon 19727
1927 heidenreich

STAATSTHEATER BERLIN

STAATS-OPER
UNTER DEN LINDEN

Dienstag, den 5. Oktober 1943
15—18¼ Uhr   Ausverkauft

DON CARLOS
Oper in vier Akten (7 Bildern) von Giuseppe Verdi

Musikalische Leitung: Robert Heger   *Spielleitung:* I. Eden

Philipp II., König von Spanien	Friedrich Dalberg
Elisabeth von Valois, seine Gemahlin	Tiana Lemnitz
Don Carlos, Infant von Spanien	Franz Völker
Prinzessin Eboli	Margarete Klose
Marquis von Posa, ein Malteserritter	Heinrich Schlusnus
Der Groß-Inquisitor	Walter Großmann
Ein Mönch (Karl V.)	Wilhelm Hiller
Eine Stimme aus der Höhe	Irmgard Langhammer
Graf von Lerma	Fritz Marcks
Tebaldo, ein Page der Königin	Vera Schröder
Ein Herold	Gustav Rödin

Flandrische Deputierte .... Hans Wrana, Franz Sauer, Felix Fleischer, Otto Hüsch, Ernst Spangenberg, Erich Pina

Herren und Damen vom Spanischen Hofe, Volk, Pagen, Leibwachen des Königs, Diener der Inquisition, Soldaten, Magistratspersonen usw.

Chöre: Gerhard Steeger   *Bühnenbilder:* Edmund Erpf
Kostüme: Kurt Palm   *Bühnentechnische Einrichtung:* Rudolf Klein

Größere Pause nach dem 4. Bild

Vor dem Vorhang erscheinen nur darstellende Künstler. Diese stellen eine Gemeinschaft innerhalb des Kunstwerkes dar; es wird deshalb gebeten, bei Beifallskundgebungen von dem Rufen einzelner Namen abzusehen.

maria müller
1898-1958

LUDWIG VAN BEETHOVEN (1770-1827)

klärchen-lieder/egmont: die trommel gerühret
berlin			raucheisen		lp: acanta 40.23535/DE 23112-23113
1943

klärchen-lieder/egmont: freudvoll und leidvoll
berlin			raucheisen		lp: acanta 40.23535
1943

JOHANNES BRAHMS (1833-1897)

feldeinsamkeit (ich ruhe still im hohen grünen gras)
london			newton			78: electrola DB 3285
24 may						78: victor 15218
1937						45: electrola E 40933
						lp: emi RLS 154 7003
						cd: preiser 89235

frühlingstrost (es weht um mich narzissenduft)
berlin			raucheisen		lp: acanta 40.23524/DE 23112-23113
1944

geheimnis (o frühlings-abenddämmerung!)
berlin			raucheisen		lp: acanta 40.23524/DE 23112-23113
1944

lerchengesang (ätherische ferne stimmen)
berlin			raucheisen		lp: acanta 40.23524
1944

das mädchen (stand das mädchen am bergesabhang)
berlin			raucheisen		lp: acanta 40.23524
1944

muss es eine trennung geben?/die schöne magelone
berlin			raucheisen		lp: acanta 40.23524/DE 23112-23113
1944

brahms **sulima (geliebter wo zaudert dein irrender fuss?)**
berlin　　　　　raucheisen　　　lp: acanta 40.23524
1944

der tod das ist die kühle nacht
berlin　　　　　raucheisen　　　lp: acanta 40.23524/DE 23112-23113
1944

zigeunerlieder
berlin　　　　　raucheisen　　　cd: preiser 89235
1944

ANTONIN DVORAK (1841-1904)

rusalka, excerpt (o silver moon!)
berlin　　　　　raucheisen　　　unpublished reichsrundfunk broadcast
1944

WOLFGANG AMADEUS MOZART (1756-1791)

don giovanni

new york 17 december 1932	*role of elvira* metropolitan opera orchestra and chorus serafin ponselle fleischer schipa pinza pasero rothier	lp: ed smith UORC 216 *heavily cut performance*
new york 20 january 1934	metropolitan opera orchestra and chorus serafin ponselle fleischer schipa pinza lazzari list	unpublished met broadcast
new york 9 february 1935	metropolitan opera orchestra and chorus ponselle fleischer borgioli pinza lazzari list	unpublished met broadcast

these performances were sung in the original italian

HANS PFITZNER (1869-1949)

sonst (es glänzt der tulpenflor)
berlin raucheisen lp: acanta 40.23532
14 may
1944

venus mater (träume, du mein süsses leben)
berlin raucheisen lp: acanta 40.23532/DE 23112-23113
14 may
1944

verrat (ich muss euch verraten)
berlin raucheisen lp: acanta DE 23112-23113
14 may
1944

GIACOMO PUCCINI (1858-1924)

la boheme
new york	*role of mimi*	unpublished met broadcast
24 december	metropolitan	
1932	opera orchestra	
	and chorus	
	bellezza	
	morgana	
	lauri-volpi	
	bonelli	
	frigerio	
	pinza	
	sung in the	
	original italian	

la boheme, excerpt (si mi chiamano mimi)
berlin	staatskapelle	78: electrola EJ 218
9 december	blech	cd: preiser 89235
1927		

la boheme, excerpt (o soave fanciulla)
berlin	staatskapelle	78: electrola EJ 217
9 december	blech	cd: preiser 89235
1927	pattiera	

la boheme, excerpt (sono andati?)
berlin	staatskapelle	78: electrola EJ 217
9 december	blech	cd: preiser 89235
1927	pattiera	

further excerpts from this live performance at the krolloper (staatsoper am platz der republik) were recorded by electrola but remained unpublished

MAX REGER (1873-1916)

waldeinsamkeit (gestern abend in der stillen ruh')
london	newton	78: electrola DB 3285
24 may		78: victor 15218
1937		45: electrola E 40933
		cd: preiser 89235
berlin	raucheisen	lp: acanta DE 23112-23113
1944		

zum schlafen (oben in dem birnbaum)
london	newton	78: electrola DB 3285
24 may		78: victor 15218
1937		45: electrola E 40933
		cd: preiser 89235
berlin	raucheisen	lp: acanta DE 23112-23113
1944		

FRANZ SCHUBERT (1797-1828)

gretchen am spinnrade (meine ruh' ist hin, mein herz ist schwer!)
berlin   raucheisen   lp: acanta DE 23112-23113
1944

heiss mich nicht reden/mignon-lieder
berlin   raucheisen   cd: preiser 89235
1944

lachen und weinen zu jeglicher stunde
berlin   rauchseisen   lp: acanta DE 23112-23113
1944

so lasst mich scheinen/mignon-lieder
berlin   raucheisen   cd: preiser 89235
1944

was bedeutet die bewegung?/suleika-lieder
berlin   raucheisen   cd: preiser 89235
1943

ROBERT SCHUMANN (1810-1856)

dein tag ist aus/byron-lieder
berlin   raucheisen   unpublished reichsrundfunk recording
1943

RICHARD STRAUSS (1864-1949)

wiegenlied (träume du mein süsses leben)
berlin   raucheisen   lp: acanta DE 23112-23113
1944

RICHARD WAGNER (1813-1883)

der fliegende holländer
bayreuth	*role of senta*	cd: preiser 90232
18 july	bayreuth	*excerpts*
1942	festival	lp: acanta 40.23502
	orchestra	cd: preiser 90364
	and chorus	cd: hamburger archiv für gesangskunst
	kraus	HAGWAGNER 2
	asmus	
	völker	
	berglund	
	hofmann	

der fliegende holländer, excerpt (traft ihr das schiff)
berlin	berlin radio	lp: acanta DE 23112-23113
1943	orchestra	cd: preiser 89235
	and chorus	
	rother	
	waldenau	

der fliegende holländer, excerpt (wie aus ferne längst vergang'ner zeiten)
berlin	berlin radio	lp: acanta 40.23502/22.220273/
1943	orchestra	DE 23112-23113
	rother	
	prohaska	

wagner **lohengrin**

new york	*role of elsa*	unpublished met broadcast
9 january	metropolitan	
1932	opera orchestra	
	and chorus	
	bodanzky	
	branzell	
	lorenz	
	schorr	
	andresen	
	cehanovsky	

berlin	staatskapelle	lp: preiser LOH 2B
31 october	and chorus	cd: preiser 90043
1943	heger	*excerpts*
	klose	lp: acanta 40.23502/98.221776/
	völker	HB 22.8630/DE 21996/
	prohaska	DE 23112-23113
	hofmann	cd: preiser 89235/90364
	grossmann	cd: hamburger archiv für gesangskunst
		HAGHOF 2/HAGWAGNER 3

lohengrin, fragment (du trugest zu ihm meine klage)

vienna	vienna	cd: koch 3-1468-2
19 june	philharmonic	*guest performance by forces of berlin staatsoper*
1938	vienna opera	
	chorus	
	berlin staatsoper	
	chorus	
	tietjen	

lohengrin, fragmentary excerpt (elsa ich liebe dich!/durch gottes sieg ist jetzt dein leben mein!)

vienna	vienna	cd: koch 3-1468-2
19 june	philharmonic	*guest performances by forces of berlin staatsoper*
1938	vienna opera	
	chorus	
	berlin staatsoper	
	chorus	
	tietjen	
	klose	
	völker	
	prohaska	
	manowarda	

wagner **lohengrin, excerpt (euch lüften die mein klagen)**
vienna	vienna	cd: koch 3-1468-2
19 june	philharmonic	*guest performance by forces of berlin staatsoper*
1938	tietjen	
	klose	
	prohaska	

lohengrin, excerpt (entweihte götter!/ortrud wo bist du?)
vienna	vienna	cd: koch 3-1450-2/3-1468-2
19 june	philharmonic	*guest performance by forces of berlin staatsoper*
1938	tietjen	
	klose	

lohengrin, excerpt (du ärmste kann wohl nie ermessen)
vienna	vienna	cd: koch 3-1468-2
19 june	philharmonic	*guest performance by forces of berlin staatsoper*
1938	tietjen	
	klose	

lohengrin, excerpt (gesegnet soll sie schreiten/nicht länger will ich dulden!)
vienna	vienna	cd: koch 3-1468-2
19 june	philharmonic	*guest performance by forces of berlin staatsoper*
1938	vienna opera chorus	
	berlin staatsoper chorus	
	tietjen	
	klose	
	manowarda	

wagner **lohengrin, excerpt (elsa erhebe dich!)**

vienna	vienna	cd: koch 3-1468-2
19 june	philharmonic	*guest performance by forces of berlin staatsoper*
1938	vienna opera	
	chorus	
	berlin staatsoper	
	chorus	
	tietjen	
	völker	

lohengrin, excerpt (das süsse lied verhallt)

bayreuth	bayreuth	lp: ed smith EJS 399
19 july	festival	lp: cetra FE 25
1936	orchestra	lp: acanta HB 22.8630/40.23502/
	furtwängler	40.23520
	völker	cd: acanta 44.1055
		cd: pilz CD 74807
		cd: grammofono AB 78515
		cd: iron needle IN 1634-1635
		original recording begins with radio announcement, act three prelude and treulich geführt
bayreuth	bayreuth	78: telefunken SKB 02052
20 august	festival	78: ultraphon H 22627
1936	orchestra	lp: telefunken HT 1/KT 11017/642.019
	tietjen	lp: preiser LV 81
	völker	cd: teldec 9031 764422/3984 269192
		cd: musica memoria 30283-30284
		cd: malibran CDRG 109
		3984 269192 is dated 29 august 1936
vienna	vienna	cd: koch 3-1468-2
19 june	philharmonic	*guest performance by forces of berlin staatsoper;*
1938	tietjen	*this version begins only at wie hehr erkenn' ich*
	völker	*unsrer liebe wesen*

wagner **lohengrin, fragment (wollt' ich dem dienst des reinen herzens/ mein gatte nein!)**

vienna	vienna	cd: koch 3-1468-2
19 june	philharmonic	*guest performance by forces of berlin staatsoper*
1938	vienna opera	
	chorus	
	berlin staatsoper	
	chorus	
	tietjen	
	völker	
	manowarda	

die meistersinger von nürnberg

bayreuth	*role of eva*	lp: ed smith UORC 266
15-24	bayreuth	lp: estro armonico EA 008
july	festival	lp: foyer FO 1043
1943	orchestra	lp: emi 1C181 01797-01801M
	and chorus	cd: laudis LCD 44008
	furtwängler	cd: dante LYS 026-029
	kallab	cd: grammofono AB 78602-78605
	lorenz	*excerpts*
	zimmermann	lp: emi 1C181 30669-30678M
	prohaska	lp: acanta DE 23112-23113/40.23502
	greindl	cd: acanta 44.1055
		cd: history 20.3090/20.3092
		cd: music and arts CD 794
		opening scene and quintet missing from original tap

die meistersinger von nürnberg, excerpt (verachtet mir die meister nicht

berlin	staatskapelle	lp: acanta HB 228630/22.220273/
1944	and chorus	40.23502
	heger	cd: music and arts CD 1068
	suthaus	
	hofmann	
	prohaska	

wagner **tannhäuser**
bayreuth	*role of*	78: columbia LX 81-98/LCX 46-63
july-	*elisabeth*	78: columbia (germany) LWX 3310-3317
august	bayreuth	78: columbia (france) LFX 112-129
1930	festival	78: columbia (usa) M 151/OP 24
	orchestra	78: columbia (argentina) 266414-266431
	and chorus	lp: emi 1C137 03130-03132
	elmendorff	cd: pearl GEMMCD 9941
	berger	cd: malibran
	jost-arden	*excerpts*
	pilinsky	78: columbia (germany) LWX 88-95
	janssen	78: columbia (usa) 9131M
	andresen	lp: electrola E 83387
		lp: emi RLS 7711/1C137 54390-54396M
		cd: preiser 89235
new york	metropolitan	unpublished met broadcast
12 january	opera orchestra	
1935	and chorus	
	bodanzky	
	manski	
	clark	
	melchior	
	bonelli	
	hofmann	

tannhäuser, excerpt (dich teure halle!)
vienna	vienna	cd: koch 3-1470-2
9 january	philharmonic	
1936	furtwängler	
berlin	berlin radio	lp: acanta HB 22.8630/DE 23112-23113
1943	orchestra	cd: minerva MNA 21
	rother	

tannhäuser, fragmentary excerpts (o stehet auf!/ich fleh' für ihn!)
vienna	vienna	cd: koch 3-1470-2
9 january	philharmonic	
1936	furtwängler	
	lorenz	

wagner **die walküre**

bayreuth 6 august 1934	*role of* *sieglinde* bayreuth festival orchestra elmendorff leider onegin völker bockelmann manowards	unpublished reichsrundfunk broadcast *rette mich maid! rette die mutter!* lp: ed smith UORC 264
berlin 10 june 1951	städtische oper orchestra fricsay buchner klose suthaus herrmann greindl	cd: myto MCD 93381

die walküre, act one

stuttgart
17-20
november
1951
	württem-
	bergisches
	staatsorchester
	leitner
	windgassen
	greindl
		lp: dg LPM 18022-18023/2548 735
		lp: decca (usa) DX 121
		excerpts
		78: dg LV 36 053/LVM 72 173/
		    LVM 72 188
		45: dg EPL 30 031/EPL 30 468/
		    EPL 30 501

die walküre, act three

london 26 may 1937	london philharmonic furtwängler flagstad bockelmann	lp: ed smith EJS 450 lp: private issue (japan) JPL 1020-1022 lp: discocorp RR 417 lp: acanta 40.23520 cd: acanta 44.1055 cd: myto MCD 91443 cd: grammofono AB 78512 cd: dante LYS 217-218 cd: music and arts CD 1035

wagner **die walküre, excerpt (labung biet' ich dem lechzenden gaumen)**
vienna	vienna	lp: ed smith EJS 451
13 february	philharmonic	cd: koch 3-1470-2
1936	furtwängler	
	völker	

bayreuth	bayreuth	lp: acanta HB 22.8630/40.23502
17 june	festival	cd: hamburger archiv für gesangskunst
1941	orchestra	HAGWAGNER 5
	tietjen	
	völker	

die walküre, fragments (weither traun kamst du des wegs/ich bin's höre mich an!)
vienna	vienna	cd: koch 3-1470-2
13 february	philharmonic	
1936	furtwängler	
	völker	

die walküre, excerpts (eine waffe lass' mich dir weisen!/der männer sippe)
vienna	vienna	cd: koch 3-1470-2
13 february	philharmonic	
1936	furtwängler	

berlin	staatskapelle	lp: acanta DE 23112-23113
1943	heger	

die walküre, excerpt (du bist der lenz)
vienna	vienna	cd: koch 3-1470-2
13 february	philharmonic	
1936	furtwängler	

die walküre, excerpt (was im busen ich barg/o süsseste wonne seligstes weib!)
bayreuth	bayreuth	78: telefunken SKB 02048
24 august	festival	78: grammophon NSKB 2048
1936	orchestra	78: ultraphon H 22623
	tietjen	78: supraphon H 22623
	völker	lp: telefunken HT 11/KT 11017
		lp: top classic TC 9043
		lp: dg 410 8541
		cd: teldec 9031 764422
		cd: musica memoria 30285-30286
		cd: malibran CDRG 109
		cd: preiser 89235

wagner **die walküre, excerpt (im lenzesmond leuchtest du hell/ ein minnetraum gemahnt auch mich)**

bayreuth	bayreuth	78: telefunken SKB 02048
24 august	festival	78: grammophon NSKB 2048
1936	orchestra	78: ultraphon H 22623
	tietjen	78: supraphon H 22623
	völker	lp: telefunken HT 11/KT 11017
		lp: top classic TC 9043
		lp: dg 410 8541
		cd: teldec 9031 764422
		cd: musica memoria 30285-30286
		cd: malibran CDRG 109

die walküre, excerpt (siegmund heiss' ich und siegmund bin ich!....to end of act one)

bayreuth	bayreuth	78: telefunken SKB 02047
24 august	festival	78: grammophon NSKB 2042
1936	orchestra	78: ultraphon H 22622
	tietjen	78: supraphon H 22622
	völker	lp: telefunken HT 11/KT 11017
		lp: scala (usa) 863
		lp: dg 410 8541
		cd: teldec 9031 764422
		cd: malibran CDRG 109

wagner **die walküre, excerpt (verweile süssestes weib!/wo bist du siegmund?)**
vienna	vienna	cd: koch 3-1470-2
13 february	philharmonic	
1936	furtwängler	
	völker	

die walküre, excerpt (fort denn eile!/o hehrstes wunder!)
vienna	vienna	cd: koch 3-1470-2
13 february	philharmonic	
1936	furtwängler	
	a.konetzni	

im treibhaus/wesendonk-lieder
london	newton	78: electrola DB 3256
24 may		cd: preiser 89235
1937		

träume/wesendonk-lieder
london	newton	78: electrola DB 3256
24 may		45: electrola E 40933
1937		lp: emi RLS 7711/1C137 54390-54396M
		cd: preiser 89235

heimkehret der edle held (eichhörnchen hinauf in die eiche!)
berlin	raucheisen	unpublished reichsrundfunk broadcast
1942		

CARL MARIA VON WEBER (1786-1826)

der freischütz, excerpt (leise leise)
berlin *role of agathe* 78: grammophon 68076
1943 städtische oper lp: decca (usa) X 112
 orchestra cd: preiser 89235
 heger

der freischütz, excerpt (und ob die wolke)
berlin städtische oper 78: grammophon 68079
1943 orchestra lp: decca (usa) X 112
 heger cd: preiser 89235

these two 78rpm sides were part of an abridged version of the opera issued by grammophon on eight records with catalogue numbers 68074-68081; other soloists were spletter, seider, grossmann, domgraf-fassbänder and greindl

HUGO WOLF (1860-1903)

als ich auf dem euphrat schiffte
berlin raucheisen lp: acanta 23.580
17 february
1943

er ist's!/mörike-lieder
berlin raucheisen lp: acanta 23.580
17 february
1943

gleich und gleich/goethe-lieder
berlin raucheisen lp: acanta 23.580
17 february
1943

nimmer will ich dich verlieren
berlin raucheisen lp: acanta 23.580
17 february
1943

ein stündlein wohl vor tag/mörike-lieder
berlin raucheisen lp: acanta 23.580
17 february
1943

verborgenheit/mörike-lieder
berlin raucheisen lp: acanta 23.580
17 february
1943

STAATSTHEATER BERLIN

STAATS-OPER
UNTER DEN LINDEN

Sonntag, den 19. Dezember 1943

12½—16 Uhr **TANNHÄUSER** Ausverkauft

und der Sängerkrieg auf Wartburg

Romantische Oper in 3 Akten von Richard Wagner (Deutsche Fassung)

Musikalische Leitung: Johannes Schüler   *Inszenierung: Heinz Tietjen*

Gesamtausstattung: Emil Preetorius

Hermann, Landgraf von Thüringen	Ludwig Hofmann
Elisabeth, Nichte des Landgrafen	Maria Müller
Tannhäuser	Ludwig Suthaus
Wolfram von Eschenbach	Heinrich Schlusnus
Walter von der Vogelweide *Ritter und Sänger*	Erich Witte
Biterolf	Walter Großmann
Heinrich der Schreiber	Karl Krollmann
Reinmar von Zweter	Felix Fleischer
Venus	Liselotte Enck
Ein Hirtenknabe	Carla Spletter
Edelknaben	Else Wenzlow
	Suse Schluppeck
	Christa Heyden
	Maria Zimmermann

Bacchanale im 1. Akt: Die gesamte Tanzgruppe

Chöre: Gerhard Steeger   *Choreographie: Lizzie Maudrik*

Bühnentechnische Einrichtung: Rudolf Klein

Größere Pause nach dem 1. und 2. Akt

Vor dem Vorhang erscheinen nur darstellende Künstler. Diese stellen eine Gemeinschaft innerhalb des Kunstwerkes dar; es wird deshalb gebeten, bei Beifallskundgebungen von dem Rufen einzelner Namen abzusehen.

Beim Klingelzeichen zum Beginn der Ouvertüre werden die Eingänge zum Zuschauerraum geschlossen

STAATSTHEATER BERLIN

STAATS-OPER
UNTER DEN LINDEN

Sonnabend, den 10. Juli 1943
18—21 Uhr   Ausverkauft

DER TROUBADOUR
Oper in acht Bildern von Giuseppe Verdi
Text nach dem Italienischen des Salvadore Cammarano

Musikalische Leitung: Robert Heger   *Spielleitung: I. Eden*

Leonore, Gräfin von Sargasto	**Tiana Lemnitz**
Ines, deren Vertraute	Irmgard Langhammer
Graf von Luna	Georg Mund a. G.
Ferrando, sein Vasall	**Wilhelm Hiller**
Azucena, eine Zigeunerin	**Margarete Klose**
Manrico	Helge Roswaenge
Ruiz, sein Freund	Fritz Marcks
Ein alter Zigeuner	Heinz Bungard
Ein Bote	Willi Fischer

Chöre: Gerhard Steeger   *Choreographie im 5. Bild: Lizzie Maudrik*

Zigeunertanz: Regina Gallo, Gerda Otto, Viola Zarell
die Herren Robst, Scheibe, Piel
Gitanilla: Gustav Blank, Jo Reinhardt, Liselotte Schmelzeisen, die Damen Mertz, Nebel, die Herren Altvater, Zobel
Tarantella: Gerda Stelzig, Rolf Jahnke, die Damen Reinhardt, Schmelzeisen, Mertz, Nebel, die Herren Blank, Altvater, Radebold, Zobel
Jota: Die Damen Gallo, Logan, Otto, Metzing, Zarell
die Herren Robst, Piel, Scheibe, Burkat, Hanschke
Finale: Die genannten Damen und Herren

Gesamtausstattung: Edmund Erpf

Bühnentechnische Einrichtung: Rudolf Klein

Kein Vorspiel — Größere Pause nach dem vierten Bild

Vor dem Vorhang erscheinen nur darstellende Künstler. Diese stellen eine Gemeinschaft innerhalb des Kunstwerkes dar; es wird deshalb gebeten, bei Beifallskundgebungen von dem Rufen einzelner Namen abzusehen.

max lorenz
1901-1975

LUDWIG VAN BEETHOVEN (1770-1828)

fidelio, excerpt (gott welch dunkel hier!/in des lebens frühlingstagen)
vienna   *role of*   unpublished acetate recording
7 january   *florestan*
1942   vienna
               philharmonic
               furtwängler

IRVING BERLIN (1888-1989)

annie get your gun, excerpt (there's no business like show business!)
vienna   orchestra   cd: myto MCD 93488
1957   paulik
               lewis
               wächter
               zimmer

GEORGES BIZET (1838-1875)

carmen, excerpt (la fleur que tu m'avais jetée)
berlin   *role of josé*   78: electrola EH 181
13 june   staatskapelle   lp: electrola E 83394
1928   schmalstich   lp: emi 1C147 29154-29155M
                                 lp: preiser LV 21
                                 cd: preiser 89232

GOTTFRIED VON EINEM (1918-1996)

der prozess
salzburg   *role of josef k*   cd: orfeo C393 952I
17 august   vienna   *world premiere performance*
1953   philharmonic
               böhm
               della casa
               hofmann
               berry
               poell

JACQUES HALEVY (1799-1862)

la juive, excerpt (quand du seigneur)
berlin	*role of eleazar*	78: electrola EH 182
13 june	staatskapelle	lp: emi 1C147 29154-29155M
1928	schmalstich	lp: preiser LV 21
		cd: preiser 89232
		cd: malibran CDRG 144

vienna	orchestra	cd: myto MCD 93488
1952	schönherr	

EUGEN HILDACH (1849-1924)

der lenz (die finken schlagen, der lenz ist da!)
berlin	staatskapelle	cd: preiser 89232
april	schmalstich	*unpublished electrola 78rpm recording*
1929		

WILHELM KIENZL (1857-1941)

der evangelimann, excerpt (selig sind die verfolgung leiden)
berlin	*role of mathias*	78: electrola EH 182
13 june	staatskapelle	lp: emi 1C147 29154-29155M
1928	schmalstich	lp: preiser LV 121
		cd: preiser 89232

RUGGIERO LEONCAVALLO (1858-1919)

i pagliacci, excerpt (un tal gioco)
berlin	*role of turiddu*	78: electrola EH 294
february	staatskapelle	cd: preiser 89232
1929	schmalstich	

vienna	orchestra	cd: myto MCD 93488
1952	schönherr	

GIACOMO MEYERBEER (1791-1864)

l' africaine, excerpt (o paradis!)
berlin	*role of vasco*	78: electrola EH 287
february	staatskapelle	lp: emi 1C147 29154-29155M
1929	schmalstich	lp; preiser LV 21
		cd: preiser 89232

HANS PFITZNER (1869-1949)

palestrina, excerpts (schlecht lohnt' ich euch; der letzte freund)
salzburg	*role of*	cd: myto MCD 92259
1 august	*palestrina*	
1955	vienna	
	philharmonic	
	kempe	
	schöffler	

CLEMENS SCHMALSTICH (1880-1960)

trinkspruch
berlin	staatskapelle	78: electrola EG 1356
april	schmalstich	lp: emi 1C147 29154-29155M
1929		lp: preiser LV 21
		cd: preiser 89232

RICHARD STRAUSS (1864-1949)

ariadne auf naxos
vienna	*role of tenor*	lp: dg LPM 18 850-18 852
11 june	*and bacchus*	lp: discocorp IGI 378
1944	vienna	lp: acanta DE 23309-23310
	philharmonic	cd: preiser 90217
	vienna opera	cd: koch 3-1473-2
	chorus	cd: arlecchino ARL 14-16
	böhm	*performance given to celebrate the*
	reining	*composer's eightieth birthday*
	seefried	
	noni	
	schöffler	

strauss **elektra**

salzburg 7 august 1957	*role of aegisth* vienna philharmonic vienna opera chorus mitropoulos borkh della casa madeira böhme	lp: concert ENAM 701 lp: discocorp SID 731 lp: cetra LO 83 cd: nuova era NE 2241-2242 cd: memories HR 4380-4381 cd: orfeo C456 972I	
vienna 1957	vienna philharmonic vienna opera chorus böhm goltz zadek klose schöffler	unpublished radio broadcast	

salome

new york 10 march 1934	*role of herod* metropolitan opera orchestra bodanzky ljungberg clemens schorr	unpublished met broadcast
munich july 1951	bavarian state orchestra keilberth borkh barth hotter	lp: melodram MEL 106 cd: orfeo C342 932I
frankfurt 9 may 1952	hessischer rundfunk orchestra schröder borkh klose frantz	cd: myto MCD 93592

220
GIUSEPPE VERDI (1813-1901)

aida
frankfurt	*role of radames*	cd: myto MCD 962.146
1952	hessischer	*excerpts*
	rundfunk	cd: myto MCD 93488
	orchestra	
	and chorus	
	kupper	
	klose	
	gonzsar	

aida, excerpt (celeste aida)
berlin	staatskapelle	78: electrola EH 181
13 june	schmalstich	lp: electrola E 83394
1928		lp: emi 1C147 29154-29155M
		lp: preiser LV 21
		cd: preiser 89232
vienna	vienna	cd: koch 3-1450-2/3-1456-2
22 september	philharmonic	
1942	ludwig	

verdi aida, excerpt (pur ti riveggo)
vienna	vienna	cd: koch 3-1456-2
22 september	philharmonic	
1942	vienna opera	
	chorus	
	ludwig	
	ilitsch	
	nikolaidi	
	alsen	
	ahlersmayer	

aida, excerpt (di miei discolpe i giudici)
vienna	vienna	cd: koch 3-1456-2
22 september	philharmonic	
1942	ludwig	
	nikolaidi	

aida, excerpt (o terra addio!)
berlin	staatskapelle	78: electrola EH 596
may	schmalstich	lp: electrola E 83394
1930	gentner-fischer	lp: emi 1C147 29154-29155M
		lp: preiser LV 121
		cd: preiser 89232
vienna	vienna	cd: koch 3-1456-2
22 september	philharmonic	
1942	ludwig	
	nikolaidi	

verdi **un ballo in maschera, excerpt (la rivedra nell' estasi)**
vienna   *role of riccardo*   cd: koch 3-1458-2
27 september   vienna
1942   philharmonic
                  böhm
                  noni

un ballo in maschera, excerpts (ogni cura si dona al diletto/ della citta all' ocaso)
vienna   vienna   cd: koch 3-1458-2
27 september   philharmonic
1942   böhm
                  noni
                  konetzni
                  nikolaidi
                  ahlersmayer

un ballo in maschera, excerpt (di tu se fedele)
vienna   vienna   cd: koch 3-1458-2
27 september   philharmonic
1942   böhm

un ballo in maschera, excerpts (e scherza e follia!/e lui! ratti movete!/ amelia tu m' ami!)
vienna   vienna   cd: koch 3-1458-2
27 september   philharmonic
1942   vienna opera
                  chorus
                  böhm
                  noni
                  konetzni
                  ahlersmayer

verdi **un ballo in maschera, excerpt (ma se m' e forza perderti)**
vienna	vienna	cd: koch 3-1458-2
27 september	philharmonic	
1942	böhm	

un ballo in maschera, fragmentary excerpts (t' amo e in lagrime/ lasciatelo! io che amai la tua consorte!)
vienna	vienna	cd: koch 3-1458-2
27 september	philharmonic	
1942	vienna opera	
	chorus	
	böhm	
	konetzni	
	noni	
	ahlersmayer	

la forza del destino, excerpt (o tu che in seno)
berlin	*role of alvaro*	78: electrola EH 287
february	staatskapelle	lp: emi 1C147 29154-29155M
1929	schmalstich	lp: preiser LV 21/LV 500
		cd: preiser 89232
vienna	orchestra	cd: myto MCD 93488
1952	schönherr	

otello, excerpt (dio mi potevi)
vienna	*role of otello*	cd: myto MCD 92260
25 november	vienna	cd: preiser 90230
1943	philharmonic	
	böhm	

otello, excerpt (poi mi giudavi?)
berlin	unknown	unpublished video recording
1943	orchestra and	*soundtrack recording only for the film*
	conductor	*altes herz wird wieder jung*
	lemnitz	

otello, excerpt (niun mi tema)
berlin	staatskapelle	cd: cantus classics CACD 500028
1943	rother	
vienna	vienna	cd: myto MCD 92260
25 november	philharmonic	cd: preiser 90230
1943	böhm	
vienna	orchestra	cd: myto MCD 93488
1952	schönherr	

RICHARD WAGNER (1813-1883)

der fliegende holländer
vienna	*role of erik*	unpublished radio broadcast
1953	vienna philharmonic	
	vienna opera chorus	
	knappertsbusch	
	goltz	
	schürhoff	
	edelmann	
	frick	

der fliegende holländer, excerpt (willst jenes tags du dich nicht mehr entsinnen?)
berlin	staatskapelle	cd: preiser 89232
march	schmalstich	cd: phonographe PHC 5016-5017
1930		*unpublished electrola 78rpm recording*
vienna	austrian radio orchestra	cd: myto MCD 93488
1948	moralt	

wagner **götterdämmerung**
bayreuth	*role of*	lp: melodram MEL 529
august	*siegfried*	cd: paragon PCD 84015-84028/
1952	bayreuth	PCD 84025-84028
	festival	
	orchestra	
	and chorus	
	keilberth	
	varnay	
	mödl	
	uhde	
	greindl	
	neidlinger	

götterdämmerung, act three
berlin	staatskapelle	cd: preiser 90245
7 november	and chorus	*excerpts*
1944	heger	lp: acanta 22.221202/22.214842
	scheppan	cd: phonographe PHC 5016-5017
	langhammer	cd: myto MCD 93592
	klose	*brünnhilde's immolation missing from this recording*
	prohaska	
	hofmann	

götterdämmerung, excerpt (zu neuen taten teurer helde!)
vienna	vienna	cd: koch 3-1474-2
24 january	philharmonic	*this version begins later at mehr gabst du wunderfrau!*
1937	knappertsbusch	
	a.konetzni	

berlin	berlin radio	cd: preiser 90451
20 october	orchestra	
1950	rother	
	braun	

götterdämmerung, excerpt (schlimmes wissen wir!)
vienna	vienna	cd: koch 3-1474-2
24 january	philharmonic	
1937	knappertsbusch	
	helletsgruber	
	michalsky	
	with	

wagner **götterdämmerung, excerpt (mime hiess ein mürrischer zwerg)**
munich	munich	78: dg LVM 72 032
19 september	philharmonic	cd: preiser 90451
1950	leitner	
	hann	

götterdämmerung, excerpts (hoiho!/von des wurmes blut mir brannten die finger/in leid zu den wipfeln/brünnhilde heilige braut!)
vienna	vienna	cd: koch 3-1474-2
24 january	philharmonic	
1937	vienna opera	
	chorus	
	knappertsbusch	
	destal	
	prohaska	

vienna	vienna	cd: koch 3-1456-2
10 september	philharmonic	*this version does not extend as far as*
1942	vienna opera	*brünnhilde heilige braut!*
	chorus	
	reichwein	
	schöffler	
	manowarda	

lohengrin
new york	*role of*	unpublished met broadcast
9 january	*lohengrin*	
1932	metropolitan	
	opera orchestra	
	and chorus	
	bodanzky	
	müller	
	branzell	
	schorr	
	andresen	
	cehanovsky	

wagner **lohengrin, excerpt (das süsse lied verhallt)**
berlin staatskapelle 78: electrola EH 406
october schmalstich lp: electrola E 83387-83388/E 83394
1929 heidersbach lp: emi 1C147 29154-29155M
              cd: phonographe PHC 5016-5017
              cd: preiser 89232
              also issued on lp by preiser

lohengrin, excerpt (atmest du nicht mit mir die süssen düfte?)
berlin staatskapelle 78: electrola EH 288
february schmalstich lp: electrola E 60591
1929   cd: preiser 89232
              also issued on lp by preiser

lohengrin, excerpt (höchstes vertrau'n hast du schon mir zu danken)
vienna austrian radio cd: myto MCD 93488
1948 orchestra
     moralt

lohengrin, excerpt (in fernem land)
vienna orchestra cd: myto MCD 93488
1953 richter

lohengrin, excerpt (mein lieber schwan)
berlin staatskapelle 78: electrola EH 288
february schmalstich lp: emi 1C147 29154-29155M
1929   lp: preiser LV 121
              cd: preiser 89232
              cd: phonographe PHC 5016-5017

wagner **die meistersinger von nürnberg**

bayreuth	*role of*	lp: ed smith UORC 266
15-24	*stolzing*	lp: estro armonico EA 008
july	bayreuth	lp: foyer FO 1043
1943	festival	lp: emi 1C181 01797-01801M
	orchestra	cd: laudis LCD 44008
	and chorus	cd: dante LYS 026-029
	furtwängler	cd: grammofono AB 78602-78605
	müller	*excerpts*
	kallab	lp: emi 1C181 30669-30678M
	zimmermann	lp: acanta 40.23502
	prohaska	cd: acanta 44.1055
	greindl	cd: history 20.3090/20.3092
		cd: music and arts CD 794

opening scene and quintet missing from original tape

die meistersinger von nürnberg, fragment (wann dann die flur vom frost befreit)

vienna	vienna	cd: koch 3-1470-2
25 november	philharmonic	
1937	furtwängler	
	wiedemann	
	krenn	
	maikl	

wagner die meistersinger von nürnberg, excerpt (am stillen herd)

berlin	staatskapelle	78: hmv C 2153
february	schmalstich	78: electrola EH 300
1929		45: electrola E 40043
		lp: electrola E 83394
		lp: emi 1C147 29154-29155M
		lp: preiser LV 121
		cd: preiser 89232
		cd: phonographe PHC 5016-5017
berlin	staatskapelle	78: electrola DB 4547
8 june	seidler-winkler	cd: preiser 89232/89404/90213
1938		cd: nimbus NI 7848
		nimbus names conductor as schmalstich

die meistersinger von nürnberg, excerpt (fanget an!)

berlin	staatskapelle	78: electrola EH 504
march	schmalstich	lp: electrola E 83394
1929		lp: emi 1C147 29154-29155M
		lp: preiser LV 121
		cd: preiser 89232
		cd: phonographe PHC 5016-5017
vienna	vienna	lp: teletheater 762.8691-762.8692
25 november	philharmonic	cd: koch 3-1470-2
1937	furtwängler	
	wiedemann	
	alsen	

die meistersinger von nürnberg, fragment (als eva aus dem paradies)

vienna	vienna	cd: koch 3-1470-2
25 november	philharmonic	*this version begins earlier at jerum! jerum!*
1937	furtwängler	
	reining	
	wiedemann	
	kamann	
vienna	vienna	cd: koch 3-1473-2
28 january	philharmonic	
1943	böhm	
	rohs	
	herrmann	

wagner **die meistersinger von nürnberg, excerpt (selig wie die sonne)**

vienna 26 february 1933	vienna philharmonic krauss ursuleac paalen zimmermann jerger	cd: koch 3-1456-2
vienna 25 november 1937	vienna philharmonic furtwängler reining szantho zimmermann wiedemann	cd: koch 3-1470-2
vienna 28 january 1943	vienna philharmonic böhm reining rohs klein herrmann	cd: koch 3-1473-2

die meistersinger von nürnberg, fragment (zeuge am ort fahret fort!)

vienna 26 february 1933	vienna philharmonic vienna opera chorus krauss ursuleac jerger zec	cd: koch 3-1456-2

wagner **die meistersinger von nürnberg, excerpt (morgenlich leuchtend)**
berlin	staatskapelle	78: electrola EH 300
20 april	viebig	lp: emi 1C147 29154-29155M
1927		lp: preiser LV 121
		cd: preiser 89232
		cd: phonographe PHC 5016-5017
vienna	vienna	cd: koch 3-1456-2
26 february	philharmonic	
1933	krauss	
vienna	vienna	lp: teletheater 762.8691-762.8692
25 november	philharmonic	cd: koch 3-1470-2
1937	furtwängler	
vienna	vienna	cd: koch 3-1473-2
28 january	philharmonic	
1943	böhm	

die meistersinger von nürnberg, excerpt (im drang der schlimmen jahr')
vienna	vienna	lp: teletheater 762.8691-762.8692
25 november	philharmonic	cd: koch 3-1470-2
1937	vienna opera	
	chorus	
	furtwängler	
	reining	
	szantho	
	zimmermann	
	kamann	
	alsen	
	wiedemann	

wagner **parsifal, excerpt (hier war das tosen!)**

berlin	staatskapelle	78: parlophone E 10477-10478
1925	and chorus	lp: emi 1C147 29154-29155M/
	s.wagner	1C137 78174-78175M
	guszalewicz	*first recording by max lorenz*

parsifal, excerpt (amfortas! die wunde!)

vienna	vienna	cd: koch 3-1472-2
10 november	philharmonic	
1942	knappertsbusch	
	braun	

parsifal, fragmentary excerpts (gelobter held!/erlösung frevlerin biet' ich auch dir/hilfe! herbei!)

vienna	vienna	cd: koch 3-1456-2
10 april	philharmonic	
1942	knappertsbusch	
	braun	
	vogel	

parsifal, excerpt (du salbtest mir die füsse)

date and	unknown	lp: discocorp IGI 379
place not	orchestra and	lp: acanta HB 22.8630
confirmed	conductor	*incorrectly described as a 1933 bayreuth festival performance conducted by strauss*
vienna	vienna	cd: koch 3-1456-2
4 april	philharmonic	
1942	reichwein	

wagner **parsifal, fragmentary excerpts (wie dünkt mich doch die aue heut' so schön!/o wehe des höchsten schmerzenstags!/ich sah sie welken, die einst mir lachten/sieh es lacht die au'!)**

date and place not confirmed	unknown orchestra and conductor	lp: discocorp IGI 379 lp: acanta 40.23502/HB 22.8630 cd: myto MCD 93488 *incorrectly described as a 1933 bayreuth festival performance conducted by strauss; singer of gurnemanz described as kipnis*
vienna 4 april 1942	vienna philharmonic reichwein roth	cd: koch 3-1456-2

parsifal, excerpt (nur eine waffe taugt!)

date and place not confirmed	unknown orchestra, chorus and conductor	lp: discocorp IGI 379 lp: acanta HB 22.8630 *incorrectly described as a 1937 bayreuth festival performance conducted by furtwängler*
vienna 4 april 1942	vienna philharmonic vienna opera chorus reichwein	cd: koch 3-1456-2

rienzi, excerpt (erstehe hohe roma neu!)

berlin 1941	*role of rienzi* staatskapelle and chorus schüler scheppan klose rödin hiller	lp: historia H 657-658 lp: acanta 72.256911/22.221202 cd: preiser 90213/90223 cd: phonographe PHC 5016-5017 *this version includes preceding chorus hoch rienzi hoch!*
vienna 24 january 1942	vienna philharmonic moralt	lp: electrola E 60591 lp: emi 1C147 29154-29155M cd: preiser 89232/89981 *unpublished electrola 78rpm recording*

wagner **rienzi, excerpt (ihr römer hört die kunde!/du friedensbote sage an!)**
berlin	staatskapelle	lp: historia H 657-658
1941	and chorus	cd: preiser 90223
	schüler	
	linde	

rienzi, excerpt (rienzi auf! schützet den tribun!/rienzi gib mir meinen vater!)
berlin	staatskapelle	lp: historia H 657-658
1941	and chorus	lp: acanta 40.23502
	schüler	cd: preiser 90223
	scheppan	
	klose	
	rödin	
	linde	
	hiller	

rienzi, excerpt (der tag ist da, die stunde naht!)
berlin	staatskapelle	lp: historia H 657-658
1941	and chorus	cd: preiser 90223
	schüler	
	scheppan	
	klose	

wagner rienzi, excerpt (allmächt'ger vater blick' herab!)

berlin	staatskapelle	78: electrola EH 504
march	schmalstich	lp: electrola E 83394
1930		lp: emi 1C147 29154-29155M
		lp: preiser LV 121
		cd: preiser 89232
berlin	staatskapelle	lp: historia H 657-658
1941	schüler	lp: acanta 22.221202
		lp: dg LPM 19 259/88 029
		cd: preiser 90213/90223
		cd: minerva MNA 21
		cd: phonographe PHC 5016-5017
vienna	vienna	lp: electrola E 60591
24 january	philharmonic	cd: preiser 89232
1942	moralt	*unpublished electrola 78rpm recording*
berlin	berlin radio	lp: acanta 40.23502
1942	orchestra	
	heger	

rienzi, excerpt (verlässt die kirche mich, zu deren preis mein werk begann?)

berlin	staatskapelle	lp: historia H 657-658
1941	and chorus	lp: acanta 40.23502
	schüler	cd: preiser 90223
	scheppan	
	klose	

rienzi, excerpt (herbei! auf eilt zu uns!)

berlin	staatskapelle	lp: historia H 657-658
1941	and chorus	cd: preiser 90223
	schüler	
	klose	

wagner **siegfried, excerpt (nothung neidliches schwert!)**

bayreuth	*role of*	78: telefunken SKB 02054
20 august	*siegfried*	lp: telefunken KT 11017
1936	bayreuth	cd: teldec 9031 764422
	festival	cd: malibran CDRG 109
	orchestra	
	tietjen	
vienna	vienna	cd: koch 3-1453-2
22 january	philharmonic	
1937	krips	
berlin	staatskapelle	78: electrola DB 4470
february	seidler-winkler	lp: electrola E 60591
1937		lp: emi 1C147 29154-29155M
		lp: preiser LV 121
		cd: preiser 89232/90213

siegfried, excerpt (schmiede mein hammer!)

bayreuth	bayreuth	78: telefunken SKB 02054
26 august	festival	lp: telefunken KT 11017
1936	orchestra	cd: teldec 9031 764422
	tietjen	cd: malibran CDRG 109
berlin	staatskapelle	78: electrola DB 4470
february	seidler-winkler	lp: electrola E 60591
1937		lp: emi 1C147 29154-29155M
		lp: preiser LV 121
		cd: preiser 89232/90213

wagner **siegfried, excerpt (dass der mein vater nicht ist!)**
bayreuth	bayreuth	78: telefunken SKB 02055
20 august	festival	lp: telefunken KT 11017
1936	orchestra	cd: teldec 9031 764422
	tietjen	cd: malibran CDRG 109
		cd: myto MCD 93488

myto edition incorrectly dated 1938 and begins only at du holdes vöglein dich hört ich noch nie!

siegfried, fragment (dein hirn brütete nicht was du vollbracht)
vienna	vienna	cd: koch 3-1474-2
16 june	philharmonic	
1937	knappertsbusch	
	zec	

siegfried, fragments (hei siegfried gehört nun der niblungen hort!/ dank liebes vöglein!/hei siegfried erschlug nun den schlimmen zwerg!)
vienna	vienna	cd: koch 3-1474-2
16 june	philharmonic	
1937	knappertsbusch	
	schumann	

siegfried, excerpt (was ihr mir nützt weiss ich nicht/hei siegfried gehört nun der helm und der ring!/er sinnt und erwägt der beute wert)
vienna	vienna	lp: ed smith EJS 444
16 june	philharmonic	cd: koch 3-1474-2
1937	knappertsbusch	
	schumann	
	wernigk	

siegfried, fragment (wie find' ich zum felsen den weg?)
vienna	vienna	lp: ed smith EJS 444
16 june	philharmonic	cd: koch 3-1474-2
1937	knappertsbusch	
	schumann	

wagner **siegfried, fragment (mein vöglein schwebte mir fort)**
vienna   vienna   cd: koch 3-1460-2
16 june   philharmonic
1937   knappertsbusch
               hofmann

siegfried, fragment (mit dem auge, das als eines mir fehlt)
vienna   vienna   cd: koch 3-1453-2
22 january   philharmonic
1937   krips
               prohaska

siegfried, closing scene (heil dir sonne!)
berlin   berlin radio   cd: preiser 90451
12 october   orchestra
1950   rother
               braun

tannhäuser, acts two and three incomplete
act two begins at freudig begrüssen wir die edle halle and act three at
ich hörte harfenschlag
berlin   *role of*   lp: acanta 22.221199/40.23502
1943   *tannhäuser*   *excerpts*
               berlin radio   lp: acanta 22.221202
               orchestra   lp: dg LPEM 19 259/88 029
               städtische   cd: preiser 90213
               oper chorus   cd: phonographe PHC 5016-5017
               rother
               reining
               bäumer
               ludwig
               schmitt-walter
               hofmann
               grossmann

wagner tannhäuser, fragment (zu ihr! o führet mich zu ihr!)
vienna	vienna	cd: koch 3-1467-2
20 november	philharmonic	cd: radio years RY 98
1937	vienna opera	
	chorus	
	knappertsbusch	
	alsen	

tannhäuser, excerpt (dir töne lob!)
berlin	staatskapelle	cd: preiser 89232
may	schmalstich	*unpublished electrola 78rpm recording*
1930		

vienna	vienna	cd: koch 3-1470-2
9 january	philharmonic	
1936	furtwängler	

tannhäuser, excerpt (o fürstin!)
berlin	staatskapelle	78: electrola EH 414
october	schmalstich	lp: preiser LV 21
1929	heidersbach	cd: preiser 89232

vienna	vienna	cd: koch 3-1470-2
9 january	philharmonic	
1936	furtwängler	
	müller	

vienna	vienna	78: electrola DB 7624
24 january	philharmonic	lp: electrola E 60591
1942	moralt	lp: emi 1C147 19154-29155M/EX 29 02123
	reining	lp: preiser LV 1315/LV 1333
		cd: preiser 89065/89232/89401/90213
		cd: emi CMS 764 0082
		also issued on a private lp by preiser

wagner **tannhäuser, fragment (erbarm' dich mein!/ich fleh' für ihn!)**

vienna 9 january 1936	vienna philharmonic vienna opera chorus furtwängler müller hofmann	cd: koch 3-1470-2
vienna 20 november 1937	vienna philharmonic vienna opera chorus knappertsbusch reining alsen	cd: koch 3-1467-2 cd: radio years RY 98

tannhäuser, excerpt (versammelt sind aus meinen landen/nach rom!)

vienna 20 november 1937	vienna philharmonic vienna opera chorus knappertsbusch reining maikl schellenberg madin gallos ettl alsen	cd: koch 3-1467-2 cd: radio years RY 98

wagner **tannhäuser, excerpt (inbrunst im herzen)**

berlin 13 march 1928	staatskapelle viebig	78: electrola EH 136 lp: preiser LV 21 cd: preiser 89232
berlin 1936	städtische oper orchestra schmidt- isserstedt	78: telefunken E 2091 lp: telefunken HT 1/KT 11017
vienna 20 november 1937	vienna philharmonic knappertsbusch	cd: koch 3-1467-2 cd: radio years RY 98 *this version begins later at von fernher tönten gnadenlieder*
berlin 8 june 1938	staatskapelle seidler-winkler	78: electrola DB 4553 lp: preiser LV 121 cd: preiser 89232/89981 *preiser cd issues describe this as an unpublished take*
vienna 31 january 1942	vienna philharmonic knappertsbusch	78: electrola DB 7602 lp: electrola E 60591 lp: emi 1C147 29154-29155M cd: preiser 89232/90116 cd: toshiba SGR 8228 *this version begins at hör' an wolfram!; also issued on lp by preiser*

wagner **tristan und isolde**

vienna 2 january 1943	*role of tristan* vienna philharmonic vienna opera chorus furtwängler a.konetzni klose, alsen schöffler	cd: koch 3-1461-2 *acts one and two are incomplete in this recording*

berlin
14-19
may
1943
	staatskapelle
	and chorus
	heger
	buchner
	klose
	hofmann
	prohaska
		lp: acanta DE 22316
		cd: preiser 90243
		cd: grammofono AB 78840-78842
		excerpts
		lp: eterna 821 028/821 029
		lp: acanta 22.223167/22.221202/
		    22.220272/98.256902/98.221776/
		    40.23502/HB 22.8630
		cd: preiser 89403/90213
		cd: phonographe PHC 5016-5017/PHC 5091
		cd: vocal archives VA 1143
		excerpt on 40.23502 (wohin nun tristan scheidet) is
		incorrectly described as being taken from 1939
		bayreuth festival and conducted by de sabata

hamburg 16 december 1949	ndr orchestra and chorus schmidt- isserstedt baumann klose herrmann kronenberg	lp: melodram MEL 444 cd: myto MCD 981.178 *excerpts* lp: royale 1353 *royale excerpts were issued using artist pseudonyms*

tristan und isolde, excerpt (o sink hernieder nacht der liebe/einsam wachend/so stürben wir um ungetrennt)

vienna 25 december 1941	vienna philharmonic furtwängler a.konetzni, klose	cd: koch 3-1456-2
munich 22 september 1950	munich philharmonic leitner goltz, wysor	78: dg LVM 72 031-72 032 cd: preiser 90451

wagner **tristan und isolde, fragments from act three** (dünkt dich das?/
das licht wann löscht es aus?/siehst du's noch nicht?)

milan	la scala	lp: ed smith UORC 260
14 april	orchestra	lp: discocorp IGI 347
1948	de sabata	
	schöffler	

die walküre

new york	*role of*	unpublished met broadcast
29 january	*siegmund*	
1949	metropolitan	
	opera orchestra	
	stiedry	
	traubel	
	bampton	
	thorborg	
	berglund	
	vichegonov	
new york	metropolitan	unpublished met broadcast
18 march	opera orchestra	
1950	stiedry	
	traubel	
	bampton	
	thebom	
	janssen	
	list	
bayreuth	bayreuth	lp: melodram MEL 547
25 july	festival	cd: melodram MEL 36102
1954	orchestra	
	keilberth	
	varnay	
	mödl	
	milinkovic	
	hotter	
	greindl	

die walküre, act one

dresden	dresden	lp: preiser 0120 015-0120 016
21 september	staatskapelle	cd: preiser 90015
1944	elmendorff	cd: tahra TAH 324-327
	teschemacher	*excerpts*
	böhme	lp: acanta 22.220281/22.221202
		cd: phonographe PHC 5016-5017

wagner **die walküre, act one scene three (ein schwert verhiess mir der vater.....to end)**

berlin	berlin radio	lp: dg LPEM 19 259/88 029
17 october	orchestra	lp: acanta DE 23.2212
1941	rother	cd: myto MCD 93488
	reining	cd: dg 459 0062/459 0662
		excerpts
		lp: acanta 22.221202/22.221229
		cd: preiser 90213
		cd: phonographe PHC 5016-5017

die walküre, fragments (wes herd dies auch sei/schmecktest du ihn mir zu?)

vienna	vienna	cd: koch 3-1469-2
unconfirmed	philharmonic	
date	martin	
	konetzni	

die walküre, fragment (kuhlende labung gab mir der quell)

vienna	vienna	cd: koch 3-1474-2
1 december	philharmonic	
1943	knappertsbusch	
	konetzni	

die walküre, excerpt (ein schwert verhiess mir der vater)

berlin	staatskapelle	78: electrola EG 860
12 march	viebig	45: electrola E 40043
1928		lp: electrola E 83394
		lp: preiser LV 21
		cd: preiser 89232

berlin	staatskapelle	78: electrola DB 4547
8 june	seidler-winkler	lp: emi 1C147 29154-29155M
1938		lp: preiser LV 121
		cd: preiser 89232/89981

wagner **die walküre, fragment (eine waffe lass mich dir weisen!)**
vienna   vienna   cd: koch 3-1474-2
1 december   philharmonic
1943   knappertsbusch
                konetzni

die walküre, excerpt (winterstürme wichen dem wonnemond)
berlin   staatskapelle   78: electrola EG 861
12 march   viebig   lp: electrola E 83394
1928   lp: emi 1C147 29154-29155M
                                    lp: preiser LV 21
                                    cd: preiser 89232

die walküre, fragments (du bist der lenz/was mich berückt errat'
ich nun leicht/siegmund! so nenn' ich dich!)
vienna   vienna   cd: koch 3-1467-2
1 december   philharmonic
1943   knappertsbusch
                konetzni

FELIX VON WEINGARTNER (1863-1942

liebesfeier (an ihren bunten liedern klettert die lerche)
berlin   staatskapelle   78: electrola EG 1356
april   schmalstich   lp: electrola E 83394
1929   lp: emi 1C147 29154-29155M
                                    lp: preiser LV 21
                                    cd: preiser 89232

STAATSTHEATER BERLIN

STAATS-OPER
UNTER DEN LINDEN

Mittwoch, den 22. September 1943

17—19½ Uhr   **Ausverkauft**

FIDELIO
Oper in zwei Akten von Ludwig van Beethoven

Zu Anfang: Ouvertüre zu „Fidelio" Vor der letzten Verwandlung: Ouvertüre „Leonore (Nr. 3)"

Musikalische Leitung: Robert Heger   *Inszenierung: Edgar Klitsch*

Don Fernando, Minister	Walter Großmann
Don Pizarro, Gouverneur eines Staatsgefängnisses	Jaro Prohaska
Florestan, ein Gefangener	Max Lorenz
Leonore, seine Gemahlin, unter dem Namen Fidelio	Paula Buchner
Rocco, Kerkermeister	Ludwig Hofmann
Marzelline, seine Tochter	Carla Spletter
Jacquino, Pförtner	Erich Zimmermann
Staatsgefangene	Gustav Rödin, Franz Sauer

Gefangene, Wachen, Volk

Chöre: Gerhard Steeger   *Bühnenbild: Berthold Adolph*

Kostüme: Edward Suhr   *Bühnentechnische Einrichtung: Rudolf Klein*

Pause nach dem ersten Akt

Vor dem Vorhang erscheinen nur darstellende Künstler. Diese stellen eine G e m e i n s c h a f t innerhalb des Kunstwerkes dar; es wird deshalb gebeten, bei Beifallskundgebungen von dem Rufen einzelner Namen abzusehen.

Beim Klingelzeichen zum Beginn der Ouvertüre werden die Eingangstüren zum Zuschauerraum geschlossen.

Discographies by Travis & Emery:
Discographies by John Hunt.

1987: 978-1-906857-14-1: From Adam to Webern: the Recordings of von Karajan.
1991: 978-0-951026-83-0: 3 Italian Conductors and 7 Viennese Sopranos: 10 Discographies: Arturo Toscanini, Guido Cantelli, Carlo Maria Giulini, Elisabeth Schwarzkopf, Irmgard Seefried, Elisabeth Gruemmer, Sena Jurinac, Hilde Gueden, Lisa Della Casa, Rita Streich.
1992: 978-0-951026-85-4: Mid-Century Conductors and More Viennese Singers: 10 Discographies: Karl Boehm, Victor De Sabata, Hans Knappertsbusch, Tullio Serafin, Clemens Krauss, Anton Dermota, Leonie Rysanek, Eberhard Waechter, Maria Reining, Erich Kunz.
1993: 978-0-951026-87-8: More 20th Century Conductors: 7 Discographies: Eugen Jochum, Ferenc Fricsay, Carl Schuricht, Felix Weingartner, Josef Krips, Otto Klemperer, Erich Kleiber.
1994: 978-0-951026-88-5: Giants of the Keyboard: 6 Discographies: Wilhelm Kempff, Walter Gieseking, Edwin Fischer, Clara Haskil, Wilhelm Backhaus, Artur Schnabel.
1994: 978-0-951026-89-2: Six Wagnerian Sopranos: 6 Discographies: Frieda Leider, Kirsten Flagstad, Astrid Varnay, Martha Moedl, Birgit Nilsson, Gwyneth Jones.
1995: 978-0-952582-70-0: Musical Knights: 6 Discographies: Henry Wood, Thomas Beecham, Adrian Boult, John Barbirolli, Reginald Goodall, Malcolm Sargent.
1995: 978-0-952582-71-7: A Notable Quartet: 4 Discographies: Gundula Janowitz, Christa Ludwig, Nicolai Gedda, Dietrich Fischer-Dieskau.
1996: 978-0-952582-72-4: The Post-War German Tradition: 5 Discographies: Rudolf Kempe, Joseph Keilberth, Wolfgang Sawallisch, Rafael Kubelik, Andre Cluytens.
1996: 978-0-952582-73-1: Teachers and Pupils: 7 Discographies: Elisabeth Schwarzkopf, Maria Ivoguen, Maria Cebotari, Meta Seinemeyer, Ljuba Welitsch, Rita Streich, Erna Berger.
1996: 978-0-952582-77-9: Tenors in a Lyric Tradition: 3 Discographies: Peter Anders, Walther Ludwig, Fritz Wunderlich.
1997: 978-0-952582-78-6: The Lyric Baritone: 5 Discographies: Hans Reinmar, Gerhard Huesch, Josef Metternich, Hermann Uhde, Eberhard Waechter.
1997: 978-0-952582-79-3: Hungarians in Exile: 3 Discographies: Fritz Reiner, Antal Dorati, George Szell.
1997: 978-1-901395-00-6: The Art of the Diva: 3 Discographies: Claudia Muzio, Maria Callas, Magda Olivero.
1997: 978-1-901395-01-3: Metropolitan Sopranos: 4 Discographies: Rosa Ponselle, Eleanor Steber, Zinka Milanov, Leontyne Price.
1997: 978-1-901395-02-0: Back From The Shadows: 4 Discographies: Willem Mengelberg, Dimitri Mitropoulos, Hermann Abendroth, Eduard Van Beinum.
1997: 978-1-901395-03-7: More Musical Knights: 4 Discographies: Hamilton Harty, Charles Mackerras, Simon Rattle, John Pritchard.
1998: 978-1-901395-94-5: Conductors On The Yellow Label: 8 Discographies: Fritz Lehmann, Ferdinand Leitner, Ferenc Fricsay, Eugen Jochum, Leopold Ludwig, Artur Rother, Franz Konwitschny, Igor Markevitch.
1998: 978-1-901395-95-2: More Giants of the Keyboard: 5 Discographies: Claudio Arrau, Gyorgy Cziffra, Vladimir Horowitz, Dinu Lipatti, Artur Rubinstein.
1998: 978-1-901395-96-9: Mezzo and Contraltos: 5 Discographies: Janet Baker, Margarete Klose, Kathleen Ferrier, Giulietta Simionato, Elisabeth Hoengen.

1999: 978-1-901395-97-6: The Furtwaengler Sound Sixth Edition: Discography and Concert Listing.
1999: 978-1-901395-98-3: The Great Dictators: 3 Discographies: Evgeny Mravinsky, Artur Rodzinski, Sergiu Celibidache.
1999: 978-1-901395-99-0: Sviatoslav Richter: Pianist of the Century: Discography.
2000: 978-1-901395-04-4: Philharmonic Autocrat 1: Discography of: Herbert Von Karajan [Third Edition].
2000: 978-1-901395-05-1: Wiener Philharmoniker 1 - Vienna Philharmonic and Vienna State Opera Orchestras: Discography Part 1 1905-1954.
2000: 978-1-901395-06-8: Wiener Philharmoniker 2 - Vienna Philharmonic and Vienna State Opera Orchestras: Discography Part 2 1954-1989.
2001: 978-1-901395-07-5: Gramophone Stalwarts: 3 Separate Discographies: Bruno Walter, Erich Leinsdorf, Georg Solti.
2001: 978-1-901395-08-2: Singers of the Third Reich: 5 Discographies: Helge Roswaenge, Tiana Lemnitz, Franz Voelker, Maria Mueller, Max Lorenz.
2001: 978-1-901395-09-9: Philharmonic Autocrat 2: Concert Register of Herbert Von Karajan Second Edition.
2002: 978-1-901395-10-5: Sächsische Staatskapelle Dresden: Complete Discography.
2002: 978-1-901395-11-2: Carlo Maria Giulini: Discography and Concert Register.
2002: 978-1-901395-12-9: Pianists For The Connoisseur: 6 Discographies: Arturo Benedetti Michelangeli, Alfred Cortot, Alexis Weissenberg, Clifford Curzon, Solomon, Elly Ney.
2003: 978-1-901395-14-3: Singers on the Yellow Label: 7 Discographies: Maria Stader, Elfriede Troetschel, Annelies Kupper, Wolfgang Windgassen, Ernst Haefliger, Josef Greindl, Kim Borg.
2003: 978-1-901395-15-0: A Gallic Trio: 3 Discographies: Charles Muench, Paul Paray, Pierre Monteux.
2004: 978-1-901395-16-7: Antal Dorati 1906-1988: Discography and Concert Register.
2004: 978-1-901395-17-4: Columbia 33CX Label Discography.
2004: 978-1-901395-18-1: Great Violinists: 3 Discographies: David Oistrakh, Wolfgang Schneiderhan, Arthur Grumiaux.
2006: 978-1-901395-19-8: Leopold Stokowski: Second Edition of the Discography.
2006: 978-1-901395-20-4: Wagner Im Festspielhaus: Discography of the Bayreuth Festival.
2006: 978-1-901395-21-1: Her Master's Voice: Concert Register and Discography of Dame Elisabeth Schwarzkopf [Third Edition].
2007: 978-1-901395-22-8: Hans Knappertsbusch: Kna: Concert Register and Discography of Hans Knappertsbusch, 1888-1965. Second Edition.
2008: 978-1-901395-23-5: Philips Minigroove: Second Extended Version of the European Discography.
2009: 978-1-901395--24-2: American Classics: The Discographies of Leonard Bernstein and Eugene Ormandy.

Discography by Stephen J. Pettitt, edited by John Hunt:
1987: 978-1-906857-16-5: Philharmonia Orchestra: Complete Discography 1945-1987

Available from: Travis & Emery at 17 Cecil Court, London, UK. (+44) 20 7 240 2129. email on sales@travis-and-emery.com .

© Travis & Emery 2009

Music and Books published by Travis & Emery Music Bookshop:
Anon.: Hymnarium Sarisburiense, cum Rubricis et Notis Musicis.
Agricola, Johann Friedrich from Tosi: Anleitung zur Singkunst.
Bach, C.P.E.: edited W. Emery: Nekrolog or Obituary Notice of J.S. Bach.
Bateson, Naomi Judith: Alcock of Salisbury
Bathe, William: A Briefe Introduction to the Skill of Song
Bax, Arnold: Symphony #5, Arranged for Piano Four Hands by Walter Emery
Burney, Charles: The Present State of Music in France and Italy
Burney, Charles: The Present State of Music in Germany, The Netherlands ...
Burney, Charles: An Account of the Musical Performances ... Handel
Burney, Karl: Nachricht von Georg Friedrich Handel's Lebensumstanden.
Cobbett, W.W.: Cobbett's Cyclopedic Survey of Chamber Music. (2 vols.)
Corrette, Michel: Le Maitre de Clavecin
Crimp, Bryan: Dear Mr. Rosenthal ... Dear Mr. Gaisberg ...
Crimp, Bryan: Solo: The Biography of Solomon
d'Indy, Vincent: Beethoven: Biographie Critique
d'Indy, Vincent: Beethoven: A Critical Biography
d'Indy, Vincent: César Franck (in French)
Frescobaldi, Girolamo: D'Arie Musicali per Cantarsi. Primo & Secondo Libro.
Geminiani, Francesco: The Art of Playing the Violin.
Handel; Purcell; Boyce; Geene et al: Calliope or English Harmony: Volume First.
Häuser: Musikalisches Lexikon. 2 vols in one.
Hawkins, John: A General History of the Science and Practice of Music (5 vols.)
Herbert-Caesari, Edgar: The Science and Sensations of Vocal Tone
Herbert-Caesari, Edgar: Vocal Truth
Hopkins and Rimboult: The Organ. Its History and Construction.
Hunt, John: Adam to Webern: the recordings of von Karajan
Isaacs, Lewis: Hänsel and Gretel. A Guide to Humperdinck's Opera.
Isaacs, Lewis: Königskinder (Royal Children) A Guide to Humperdinck's Opera.
Kastner: Manuel Général de Musique Militaire
Lacassagne, M. l'Abbé Joseph : Traité Général des élémens du Chant.
Lascelles (née Catley), Anne: The Life of Miss Anne Catley.
Mainwaring, John: Memoirs of the Life of the Late George Frederic Handel
Malcolm, Alexander: A Treaty of Music: Speculative, Practical and Historical
Marx, Adolph Bernhard: Die Kunst des Gesanges, Theoretisch-Practisch
May, Florence: The Life of Brahms
May, Florence: The Girlhood Of Clara Schumann: Clara Wieck And Her Time.
Mellers, Wilfrid: Angels of the Night: Popular Female Singers of Our Time
Mellers, Wilfrid: Bach and the Dance of God
Mellers, Wilfrid: Beethoven and the Voice of God
Mellers, Wilfrid: Caliban Reborn - Renewal in Twentieth Century Music

Music and Books published by Travis & Emery Music Bookshop:
Mellers, Wilfrid: François Couperin and the French Classical Tradition
Mellers, Wilfrid: Harmonious Meeting
Mellers, Wilfrid: Le Jardin Retrouvé, The Music of Frederic Mompou
Mellers, Wilfrid: Music and Society, England and the European Tradition
Mellers, Wilfrid: Music in a New Found Land: ... ... American Music
Mellers, Wilfrid: Romanticism and the Twentieth Century (from 1800)
Mellers, Wilfrid: The Masks of Orpheus: ...... the Story of European Music.
Mellers, Wilfrid: The Sonata Principle (from c. 1750)
Mellers, Wilfrid: Vaughan Williams and the Vision of Albion
Panchianio, Cattuffio: Rutzvanscad Il Giovine
Pearce, Charles: Sims Reeves, Fifty Years of Music in England.
Playford, John: An Introduction to the Skill of Musick.
Purcell, Henry et al: Harmonia Sacra ... The First Book, (1726)
Purcell, Henry et al: Harmonia Sacra ... Book II (1726)
Quantz, Johann: Versuch einer Anweisung die Flöte traversiere zu spielen.
Rameau, Jean-Philippe: Code de Musique Pratique, ou Methodes.
Rastall, Richard: The Notation of Western Music.
Rimbault, Edward: The Pianoforte, Its Origins, Progress, and Construction.
Rousseau, Jean Jacques: Dictionnaire de Musique
Rubinstein, Anton : Guide to the proper use of the Pianoforte Pedals.
Sainsbury, John S.: Dictionary of Musicians. Vol. 1. (1825). 2 vols.
Serré de Rieux, Jean de : Les dons des Enfans de Latone
Simpson, Christopher: A Compendium of Practical Musick in Five Parts
Spohr, Louis: Autobiography
Spohr, Louis: Grand Violin School
Tans'ur, William: A New Musical Grammar; or The Harmonical Spectator
Terry, Charles Sanford: J.S. Bach's Original Hymn-Tunes for Congregational Use.
Terry, Charles Sanford: Four-Part Chorals of J.S. Bach. (German & English)
Terry, Charles Sanford: Joh. Seb. Bach, Cantata Texts, Sacred and Secular.
Terry, Charles Sanford: The Origins of the Family of Bach Musicians.
Tosi, Pierfrancesco: Opinioni de' Cantori Antichi, e Moderni
Van der Straeten, Edmund: History of the Violoncello, The Viol da Gamba ...
Van der Straeten, Edmund: History of the Violin, Its Ancestors... (2 vols.)
Waltern: Musikalisches Lexicon
Walther, J. G.: Musicalisches Lexikon ober Musicalische Bibliothec

Travis & Emery Music Bookshop
17 Cecil Court, London, WC2N 4EZ, United Kingdom.
Tel. (+44) 20 7240 2129
© Travis & Emery 2009